JUNGLE BABY

A MEMOIR

ALIDA ALBERT

Table of Contents

To my loving family, Bruce, Jenny and Kim.
Thanks for all the support and encouragement
you've given me over the past few years as I
wrote this book. Thanks especially to Kim,
who bought me at least one book about memoir
writing and gave me that extra push I needed
to finally get it done.

Preface

Africa, that most exotic and exciting of all the continents…everything in my early life is remembered by whether it occurred before, during or after Africa.

This is my story, but it's also the story of my parents, told in their voice thanks to recalled conversations, letters and short stories that I unearthed from files that were in my basement. I have my memories, and I have my story, no regrets. As for my father, I have no anger, just curiosity about his decision-making process. I know my parents loved me, which is what makes it all so hard to understand.

Born in the early 1900s, some of the words and thoughts expressed by my father might not be said in this age of political correctness. While they may sound racist to some, that's a word I would never use to describe him. He was simply a product of his time and a colorful character. He didn't have animosity toward someone because of his race or religion—rather, he disdained people he considered stupid, and that could include anyone and everyone.

Grownups like to say
That children are resilient.
That's what they say
To help themselves excuse the inexcusable
And justify the unjustifiable.

Alida Albert

Chapter 1

❦ ❦ ❦ ❦ ❦ ❦

Leaving Africa—March 1953

It was just after sunup and we were driving in an old red pickup truck that my father borrowed from a friend. He had sold our shiny black Buick convertible with the red leather upholstery and power windows to an African chief for twenty tons of galena. An African was driving, I was in the middle because I was only ten and needed less legroom my mother said, and she was next to the window. My father was sitting on a bench in the back of the truck with our suitcases. We had just left the Pax Hotel, our home in Jos for the past year, and Ginger, the marmalade-colored cat I loved so dearly.

My parents had been planning for several months to leave Nigeria, where we had been living for two years, and return to America. At last we were driving to the airport in Kano. The airport in Jos was much closer, but my father was in a financial dispute with Barclays Bank. He was afraid that if they got wind of his impending departure they would prevent us from leaving, so he decided it would be better to quietly drive to Kano, about two hundred miles north.

A half hour out of Jos and we were into unfamiliar territory. The truck moved slowly along the dirt road, kicking up dust. There were no villages, almost no trees, a few women walking with bundles on their heads in the flat, dry terrain, and an occasional anthill five or six feet high. Made out of the saliva of ants mixed with dirt, they were so strong and hard, like baked clay, that a man could climb on them. You wouldn't want to because, while some were abandoned, most were thriving colonies of constant activity and the ants would eat you alive, right down to the bone. We passed a pack of bush dogs, feral and as dangerous as a pack of wolves, and an occasional dog-faced baboon, as big as a man and capable of a vicious attack.

It was the dry season and the land was golden from lack of rain. Even at that early hour the sun was hot. The air shimmered the road in front of us until we got right up to it and then it appeared to straighten out. A lorry passed us going in the other direction. We had been driving for what seemed like hours when we decided to stop by the side of the road and eat lunch. The owner of the Pax Hotel had packed a lunch of dry mutton sandwiches, some juicy papayas, and avocados. "I'm glad I'll never have to eat mutton again once we're back in America," I told my mother.

After lunch I asked to go to the bathroom, but there was no restroom. There was a field with high grasses taller than I was and my mother told me to go into the field. I hesitated, scared to go in alone, but there was a narrow footpath and I followed it. Now I could no longer see the road or anything but yellow grass and blue sky. A buzzard circled overhead and there was a constant high-pitched sound of insects coming from a pile of manure with dozens of flies swarming around it. Pagan, I wondered? Or could it be lion feces? We had passed some pagans earlier in the day. The men wore shirts and shorts like other African men, but the women were naked except for some leaves at their crotch. I had heard stories about attacks by leopards and lions and my heart was pounding. As soon as I could, I ran back to the car.

After we had been driving for a while we saw a village of round mud huts with thatched roofs and bright green vegetation. My first oasis. We drove by the village, but realized that we should have asked for water, because soon our truck rolled to a stop. Our driver opened the hood and tinkered with the engine.

"Sah," he reported, "the battery needs water."

The only water we had was for drinking, but it was more important to give it to the truck than keep it for us. Reluctantly, my father handed him our thermos. After the driver added water to the battery it still wouldn't start. He poked about in the back of the truck and, on the floor, he found a nail, which he pounded into the battery. Miraculously, the engine started up. Now we didn't have enough drinking water.

We drove on hour after hour and the sun began to set as we neared the outskirts of Kano. It was getting close to our flight departure time and my parents were tense because we should have been at the airport by then. I was excited to be going home and the thought of missing our flight was almost unbearable.

It was getting quite a bit more populated and it would have been good to have lights on the truck to see where we were going, but for some reason, they wouldn't go on. This really slowed us up as we were afraid of hitting the people who were riding their bicycles or walking on the side of the road. It was the common wisdom that if a white man hit an African he mustn't stop until he reached the police station to report it or the people would kill him.

Then, off in the dark there was a startling sight—a Ferris wheel, lit up and turning in the southern Sahara Desert, white lights sparkling, huge, dwarfing all the lights and buildings around it. Because we were moving slowly and cautiously without our headlamps, we had a long time to view this unexpected and magical sight.

When we arrived at the airport we were upset to discover that we had missed our BOAC flight to England by less than an hour because of the battery mishap. There was no choice but to stay at the airport hotel for the night. After we checked in we ordered dinner at the outdoor restaurant. The air was so hot and dry that by the time the bread and butter arrived at the table the bread was dried out and the butter was melted.

After dinner we were back in our room and undressed

when, about ten o'clock, there was a loud banging on the door.

"Who is it?" my father said.

"Police! Open up!"

My father opened the door and two African policemen, dressed in tan Bermuda shorts and military-style jackets, were standing there.

"Sah, you come with us to police station."

"What for?" My father sounded worried and angry.

"Sah, you come with us! They tell you there."

My father hurriedly changed from his pajamas and then he was gone. If only we had been able to catch our plane! I expected my mother to panic when he left, but outwardly at least, she remained calm and after a while I fell into a fitful sleep. I dreamt of my father and what might be happening to him, and worried about why they had taken him away and if he'd ever come back.

He returned about eight o'clock the next morning, looking wrung out and exhausted. My mother and I were already dressed and packed, and relieved to see him. There was no time for conversation because now it was a question whether we could still catch the early plane to London. We dragged our luggage out of the hotel and onto the airfield. The plane was still on the tarmac and we boarded it. When we were settled in our seats, my father said, "I wrote a check to Barclays Bank and they released me."

My mother looked at him. She didn't have time to say anything before he dismissed her silent question with a matter-of-fact statement. "The bank caught wind of our departure." He fastened his seatbelt.

"I'll stop payment when we arrive in London," he added and then turned to the window as we lifted off. "I had a hell of a night."

Chapter 2

Fateful Decisions

Way back in 1924, an enterprising adventurer from Chicago named Strickler arrived in the Gold Coast colony in British West Africa. He contrived to have himself appointed as the agent for the Gold Coast Farmers Association, comprised of over five thousand native cocoa growers. Under the terms of their agreement, Strickler was to sell their cocoa in New York.

After the cocoa was shipped, but before the farmers had received their final payment, Strickler bribed a local doctor to invalid him out of the country. He calmed the fears of the Farmers Association by telling them that it would be death for him to remain any longer in an area known as the White Man's Graveyard, but that they were to send their secretary with him to England, where he would get the balance due them and settle up. He magnanimously offered to pay the secretary's passage and the farmers consented.

Strickler and the secretary sailed on the next Elder Dempster steamer for Liverpool. The ship stopped first at Southampton, where Strickler left it under the pretext that he was going to visit a student at Oxford. That was the last the secretary ever saw of him.

In 1929, the Gold Coast Farmers Association retained a small New York law firm to help recover the balance due them. The action wasn't able to be settled until after World War II and the farmers received a little over half of what they were due.

Importers from all over West Africa began to write to the New York lawyer that they had heard about the wonderful thing he had done for the cocoa farmers and would he please help them as well. They wanted to sell mahogany, fibers, rubber, and spices and they needed help arranging to purchase bicycles, shoes, textiles, flour, roofing sheets, and everything else that post-war England was not yet able to supply them with. The lawyer threw the letters aside, saying he could not bother with matters so remote from the practice of law.

Fifteen years after graduating from Yale Law School, my father was working for the law firm that had represented the farmers. Samples of native handicrafts that the tradesmen had sent to the lawyer lay on shelves and in corners, neglected. My father was fascinated by the foreign stamps and postmarks on the letters, and intrigued by the aromatic gingerroots, the dried kola nuts, the mahogany samples, and the colorful mats that lay around the office. He decided that he wanted to trade with Africa.

Since earlier in his career he had worked in Foreign

Funds Control of the Treasury Department in Washington, D.C., he already knew a smattering of information about foreign currency and exchange. He studied the fundamentals of foreign trade from a pamphlet that he bought from the Department of Commerce for ten cents. From that slim booklet he launched a new career.

My father discovered that there is a directory in the library for almost anything you want to buy or sell. He wrote to buyers in British West Africa, gathering information about what they wanted, and at the end of three months he made his first shipment, cement, to a Nigerian trader. This was followed by a shipment of kerosene, flour, and aluminum roofing sheets. He was on his way to calling himself a foreign trader. But after the fourth shipment, the requests for goods stopped, because the British insisted the Africans had to buy from them, not Americans.

Bitten by the romance of running his own business in exotic faraway places, my father investigated importing West African products to America. He learned that importing from Africa had its limitations because agricultural produce is seasonal, but more serious was the unreliable African shippers. Often they didn't have the goods they offered to sell, but would go out to buy them only after they had your irrevocable letter of credit. They would then discover that the goods cost more than they expected, so they didn't have the necessary capital to purchase them, or that they weren't available at all.

Undaunted by every disappointment, he was continually receiving all kinds of samples and offers from native traders. One day he received a nugget of shiny mineral in the mail. After having it analyzed by an assayer he learned that it was the best galena in the world. Galena is the mineral name for the ore of lead. Further investigation disclosed that he could sell all of the ore he could possibly buy and, at the price offered, make more than a fair profit.

This was it. This would be his next flyer.

The shipper offered ten tons and wanted a letter of credit from my father, which would be valid for thirty days. Several delays and six months later, three tons arrived. However, when the ore was assayed, it exceeded all my father's hopes and yielded a profit of one hundred percent.

A one hundred percent profit was good, but not if you had to wait six months for it and tie up money for that length of time. He realized that in order to make importing financially worthwhile, it was necessary to get larger and more frequent shipments and the way to get them was to stop writing letters and making contracts with "savages." For my father it was an easy decision. He would go to the place where the ore was produced, and with cash, buy as much as he could get. His African supplier might have difficulty in getting shipping space, but my father wouldn't. The European steamship agents might ignore an African, but they wouldn't ignore my father because he was white and articulate. He could make a fuss if necessary, he was American, and he had dollars.

After my father pinpointed the areas in Nigeria where the ore came from, he wrote to the only reliable Nigerian trader he knew, a man he had done some deals with named Animashaun. My father arranged for him to travel to a remote area in the bush to determine how many tons of galena a month my father could count on and at what price.

Animashaun's encouraging reply said that he knew about mining and he assured my father that galena was plentiful in Nigeria. He said my father would easily be able to get everything that he needed. Armed with this information, my parents sat down for a serious discussion about living in Africa for an extended period of time. My father decided he would temporarily give up law and try to make his fortune as a lead and tin miner.

My mother, always very supportive, tried to suppress her trepidations—but Africa! It meant leaving her life in America, her sister, with whom she was extremely close, her two nieces and her two best friends. And what would they do with me, their only child?

"Well," my father said, "we can put the kid in boarding school in England for a while. She'll be fine. Children are resilient. She can be a tough kid to handle. And boarding school might give her some polish. If we find a school for her in Africa, we'll send for her," he consoled my mother.

But, my mother worried, would I really be all right in England, so far from them? She was uncomfortable—I wasn't even eight years old.

And what would the two of them be going to? Where would they live? What would they do with all their stuff and what about the two cats? Would it be safe in Africa?

However, she was afraid of losing my father. Their relationship was fraught with conflict and my father's behavior was the main source of the arguments. While they loved each other and she supported his various endeavors to make a living, he was a very difficult man to live with. In 1949 when he sailed to Sweden for a three-month trip to sell oil burners to a man in Stockholm, she had enclosed a tender and loving note in his suitcase, wishing him luck and telling him she would take good care of their child and that, come what may, she would always love him. He repaid her love and devotion by having an affair in Copenhagen with a woman named Margaret and then coming home and telling my mother about it, completely devastating her.

I believe it was mainly because of the affair that my mother felt that she needed to agree to the plan, and that it might even turn out to be an adventure and perhaps they would come home rich. My parents felt strongly that a wife should accompany her husband wherever he had to go to make a living. My father was prepared to venture, get dirty, be uncomfortable, and risk his money, and he expected that he would reap a commensurate reward.

In the weeks after their discussion, my father began to line up financing with the two partners of his law firm, one of whom was the lawyer who had represented the farmers. They, too, were interested in foreign trade, and agreed to pay for our fare over, our living expenses, and for purchases of raw materials.

Safe in my room, playing with my dolls while my parents planned our future, I was unaware that the somewhat heated discussions that I couldn't understand were the crack in the earth that was about to suck me down and take us all on the journey of a lifetime.

Chapter 3

Arrival in England—March 1951

I was almost eight years old, sitting on a stack of telephone books piled on the floor next to a disconnected telephone in our apartment that was echoing with emptiness. The phone books were all that remained of our life in Jackson Heights, New York. Everything else that used to be in the apartment was gone—packed, tossed out, or in storage. Our beloved cats, silky black Topsy and Dinah, a calico, had been sent to heaven. My mother said they had been "put to sleep."

We were leaving America to go live in Nigeria, British West Africa. Coincidentally, my best friend, Susan, was also going overseas, to live in Palestine with her mother and her father, who worked for the United Nations. Over the past couple of months we had been going together with our mothers to get inoculations for smallpox, yellow fever, typhoid, paratyphoid, tetanus, and bubonic plague.

At the first visit Susan went in ahead of me for her shot and came out bawling. That settled it—I was most definitely *not* going to cry, no matter how much it hurt, and I didn't. After that, neither of us cried.

Now the only things left in the apartment were us—my mother, father, me, and our suitcases—and it was time to leave. The taxi was waiting downstairs at the curb to take us to the airport. I cried all the way to the airport, sobbing how much I would miss Susan and my other best friend, Helen, and my two cousins, Helen and Jeannie.

Then we were on the plane and the engines were throbbing and we were taxiing down the runway. As the plane lifted off, the tune "Off We Go into the Wild Blue Yonder" came into my mind. When I pressed my head against the tiny window, I saw what looked like an enormous map below us and what was probably a shadow from the clouds but looked to me like a giant bent over, drawing the map.

We arrived in London the next morning and checked in at a hotel. I knew nothing of World War II and the bombing of London but I got a sense of it while we were walking around the cold, damp streets. There were buildings, intact and pretty in the front with no outside wall in the back, their rooms open to the world like a dollhouse—many buildings—what was left of the city after the Germans had bombed it.

One evening we were dining in a fancy London restaurant with starched white tablecloths and sparkling wineglasses and heavy luminous silverware lined up at each place setting. The band began to play a samba and my parents excused themselves and got up to dance. A couple at the next table noticed I was alone and asked the waiter to bring me a bowl of very expensive out-of-season strawberries. "On us," the man said to the waiter. When my parents came back the man at the other table stood up ceremoniously and, with a warm smile and a British accent, introduced himself as Michael Lyons. "And this is my wife, Joanne," he continued. "I do hope you don't mind that we sent some strawberries to your daughter."

"Not at all," my father smiled. "She seems to be enjoying them. That was very kind of you."

My father lightly draped his arm around my mother's shoulder to pull her into the conversation. "I'm Lee Franklin and this is my wife, Josephine. This young lady eating your delicious strawberries is our daughter, Alida."

"We're on our way to Nigeria, and we're here looking for a school for Alida. We're trying to find the warmest one—most of them are so chilly at this time of year," my mother said.

Mr. Lyons nodded with understanding and soon after appetizers and a lot of chatting across tables, they accepted my father's invitation to join us. Though I had no idea what he meant, Mr. Lyons said that he and his wife would like to visit me at my school and take me out for a day. My father replied, "Thank you. That would be very nice. We'll be in touch and let you know where she is."

While we spent the next several days traveling throughout London, visiting schools, Windsor Castle, and the Tower of London, it was all a big adventure to me, an interlude before we embarked as a family to our final destination, Nigeria.

One morning, bright and early, we boarded a train, climbing into a cozy first class compartment with scratchy blue mohair upholstered seats, then chugging out of London into the beautiful English countryside. I watched the gently rolling slopes and farmland going by. Patchwork fields were dotted with grazing sheep. When we arrived at our stop, the sign over the station door read "Sevenoaks, Kent."

"Take us to Farnaby School, please," my father said to the taxi driver after we had climbed down the long iron steps of the train to the platform. I snuggled between my parents, sinking into the worn-out leather in the funny square car that was driving on the wrong side of the road.

As we drove through the little town, I got a glimpse of fairytale houses and long, narrow country roads lined with tall boxwoods. Eventually the driver slowed and made his way down a long gravel driveway. He came to a stop in a circle in front of the shiny black paneled door of a large brick house with tall mullioned windows. I was entranced by its neatly landscaped garden.

My mother rang the bell and then she banged the brass lion's head door knocker. The door opened and a tall solemn woman with a stern voice invited us in. "How do you do. You must be the Franklins. I'm Mrs. French, the headmistress," and she held out her hand to shake. Then she turned to me.

"And you must be Aleeda. It's very nice to meet you," she said.

My father jumped in before I could answer. "Actually, it's pronounced Alida, with a long 'i'," he said.

"What a lovely and unusual name—what's the origin of Alida?"

"We knew someone very special," my mother replied. "An old Quaker lady named Alida Taylor. We admired her and hoped our Alida would live to be an old lady, also."

"Well, it's a lovely name and one I'll never forget," and with that Mrs. French swept us into the drafty center hall, leading us up the wide staircase to her private sitting room. It was cozy with cabbage-rose wallpaper and comfortable upholstered furniture. She closed the door and when we were all seated, she folded her hands primly in her lap and proceeded to talk about Farnaby.

"Farnaby is steeped in history and in proper traditions for children. We have good values, and all the children are C of E, of course," she said emphatically.

My father looked puzzled for a moment and then he realized that "C of E" was the Church of England. "Of course," he replied.

They talked and I fidgeted quietly as I looked around the room, not really listening. Finally, Mrs. French stood up, smiled politely and left the room. My father stood up, too, and bent down to kiss me.

"Good-bye, Dixiebelle," he said. His wool jacket scratched my cheek as he gave me a long hug. I saw my mother slipping on her leopard coat over her dress. Her eyes were moist as she kissed and hugged me.

"We love you," she said and then, just as suddenly and

unexpectedly as they had embraced me in the middle of Mrs. French's sitting room, they closed the door behind them, leaving me standing there.

Something made me run over to the window, getting there just in time to look down on the driveway and see my parents get back into the waiting taxi. In shock, I watched the doors close and the taxi turn around the circle and slowly disappear down the long driveway, away from the school and away from me.

And that was the first moment I realized I was staying at Farnaby and they were going. For two months my parents and I had been getting inoculations to go to Africa. Of course I was going with them. To the best of my recollection, school in England had never been discussed with me. And even though my parents and I had been visiting schools, my first inkling that I wouldn't be going with them was when I looked down from Mrs. French's sitting room and watched them drive away. Certainly there hadn't been any talk about how long I would be there.

"I want my mother and father," I cried out as Mrs. French walked back into the room. An annoyed look crossed her face.

"Shush," she admonished and squeezed my arm. I became more upset, hysterical, yelling and resisting whatever she was saying. Then I remembered seeing my father give her money. "I want my money," I yelled in a desperate attempt to gain some control over the situation. I felt it was my right to have it and it would be a small victory for me.

"You can't have it," she replied, and when I continued my demands for the money she stopped answering. In the hall outside Mrs. French's sitting room I stepped up the volume and began kicking and screaming, first standing up and then lying on the floor, beating the heels of my oxfords into the oak floorboards.

"You stinker," I wept loudly. "Give me my money! It's *my* money! Give it to me!" I knew I shouldn't be acting like this, but I didn't care.

Nervously, Mrs. French backed away, pained disapproval and disdain for the ill-behaved American child written all over her face, leaving me alone, thrashing and weeping on the floor of the echoing hallway. When my parents called from the train station to check up on me she said, "I want you to take your daughter out of Farnaby! She yelled at me and she even called me a stinker! I won't have that here."

He told me later, like it was a funny joke, that he answered, "In America stinker is a term of endearment."

Maybe the school really needed the money, or improbably, she believed him, because she relented.

When I had finally cried myself out, I stood up, red-eyed and exhausted. Someone else appeared and led me up a narrow flight of stairs to a room on the third floor. It was a tiny space in the attic, with a sloping ceiling and a small window. I lay down on the little bed as the tears began again.

Chapter 4

Farnaby

I don't know if it's possible for anyone to cry as much as I remember crying. For years I believed that I cried all alone in that attic room at Farnaby for three days, trying to make sense of what had happened to me. Probably, that wasn't the case because I would have gotten dressed, eaten, and gone to classes, but all I can remember is that I cried for three days.

I arrived at Farnaby in the middle of the second half of third grade and was placed with the other seven- and eight-year-olds. I was immediately thrown into the English curriculum and the strict English discipline and style of teaching. When the teacher walked into the classroom, we were already there, waiting. As one, we would rise and say in unison, "Good morning, sir."

A short, stocky, middle-aged man with gray hair, wearing a jacket and striped tie, he surveyed us unsmilingly. "Be seated," he would say.

The girls terrified me when they told me they had caning at the school, so I watched carefully to see what they were doing and I followed their lead. When the lesson began, it was more like we wanted to encourage the teacher than the other way around. As he explained math, the girls, most sitting with one leg tucked beneath them, would lean forward attentively in their seats and say, "Oh, yes, sir. Oh, I see, sir," throughout the lesson. I sat the way they did and echoed their "Oh, I see, sirs" even if I didn't "see" his explanation. And, like the other girls, I wore the school uniform of an itchy gray flannel skirt and jacket with a white blouse beneath it.

Each school day began with a prayer service following breakfast. Every Sunday morning we shined our brown oxfords for the weekdays, and our black oxfords for Sunday church services. One time, we even shined the soles of our black oxfords, which made for a pretty slippery walk to the magnificent old stone church just down the road.

After what seemed like forever living alone in the attic, I was assigned to a room one flight down, on the same floor as all the other girls. I now had two roommates. Beatrice and I were the same age and Carol was a year older. On the first night, Carol announced, "I know a really fun game."

We waited for her to describe anything that sounded like fun. Beatrice and I wanted to have fun.

"You lie on the bed and I jump on your stomach."

It didn't sound like fun to me, but Carol was older, and it didn't seem like we could get out of playing. So

Beatrice and I lay down on our beds and Carol took a running jump and landed on Beatrice's stomach. A loud gasp echoed through the room, and then absolute quiet. I was scared.

"That feels good. Do it again," Beatrice rasped.

So Carol did it again and again, and the whole time Beatrice kept whispering, "That feels good."

When it was my turn, Carol backed up as far across the room as she could get. I closed my eyes. I could feel her coming at me with full force. When she reached my bed she flung herself through the air and landed with a crashing thud on my chest and stomach. The air was crushed out of my body. The pain was excruciating and I nearly threw up.

"That feels good, Carol," I managed to gasp. "Do it again."

By the third time, Carol was beginning to tire of the game but not before she got in a few more jumps. I wished I could tell my mother that Carol was hurting me and she should make her stop. I knew she would be mad at Carol and would protect me if she was there. She always protected me.

The next night Carol had invented another game. This time it involved putting a pillow over Beatrice's face and sitting on it. Carol pulled up a corner of the pillow and asked, "Can you breathe? You can breathe," she said, answering her own question. After a few minutes on Beatrice's face it was my turn. The pillow over my face with the weight of Carol on top cut off all the air. I couldn't catch my breath. Carol lifted up a corner.

"You can breathe," she said. I struggled to get her off me, but she kept insisting I was all right. Finally, when it seemed like I might die, she lifted the pillow.

"That was fun," I gasped. I knew I had to show I was a good sport. I could never complain and I would never tell on her. "Mommy, help me," I prayed silently.

A few nights later, Carol generously offered Beatrice and me some candy. She took out a smallish cobalt blue bottle that said Phillip's on the front and counted out ten little white candies for each of the three of us. They tasted chalky and minty, but they weren't too bad. We ate them all. Sometime during the night I was awakened by a rumbling stomach, followed by the most intense stomach cramps I had ever experienced, and when I ran to the bathroom, I met my two roommates there with the same symptoms. The three of us spent that night and all the next day running to the bathroom. My mother would have warned me what would happen if I ate ten milk of magnesia tablets.

But Carol had a sweet side, too, and at night she'd sing:

Nightie, nightie and sweet repose
And mind the mosquitoes don't bite your toes.

Since the other girls at Farnaby also missed their parents, at bedtime we would say to each other, "Pleasant dreams and dream of your mother and father." There was some small comfort in knowing the rest of them missed their parents too, and I wasn't the only one.

Mrs. French arranged for a school trip to Windsor Castle. I had already been there with my parents before they left for Africa. I decided I didn't want to go to the castle. To make my point, I showed the nurse some spots on my body that looked like the German measles that happened to be going around the school. The nurse said the spots were nothing, but repeated showings either convinced her that I did actually have the measles or else she just gave up. In any event, I didn't go. When I finally got my way I was sorry that I hadn't gone. Everyone who wasn't sick went and had a good time, but the point was that I had gotten my way in something, a small measure of control where I had absolutely none.

One day on my way to my room, I noticed an awful smell in the upstairs hall. A teacher was seated at a small table with a line of girls standing in front of her. The odor was cod liver oil and they expected us to *voluntarily* line up for a dose of it. I considered that option for about half a minute, then decided there was no way I was going to put that vile-smelling stuff into my mouth. My mother had never given me cod liver oil. What on earth was it for? I was going to have to avoid the area where they were dispensing it. That meant in order to get from one side of the second floor to the other, I had to sneak down the back stairs to the first floor and then up the front staircase. This went on for several days until they had finished doling out the cod liver oil. I lived in dread that someone would notice that I hadn't lined up for my dose, but no one did.

As the weeks wore on, I adjusted somewhat to life at Farnaby, even though the girls made fun of my American accent. I sensed that they weren't really trying to be mean—they just didn't get how all alone I felt.

I made a friend named Daphne and was invited for a long weekend visit at her home. Her mother came for us in a large car and on our way to her house, Daphne announced, "We have sixty-four beds."

My jaw dropped. "No, darling," her mother corrected. "We have sixty-four *flower* beds."

Her home was a beautiful English stone manor house with a field full of bright white daisies in back. Beyond the daisies were woods with thousands of bluebells. Even though I was a little girl, I knew these people were rich, with their huge house and its many large rooms. Exploring the house and playing in the woods with Daphne was the happiest time I'd had since arriving in England, but they took me back to Farnaby a day early. What had I done and why would they take me so soon when I was having a good time?

When another friend invited me to her home in Bath, her mother put us in separate bedrooms although I would rather have shared a room. I cheered up a little when I saw that there was a copy of *Peter Pan* in my room. I asked if I could read it in bed before I went to sleep. Her mother said yes, but she seemed annoyed since she wanted lights out immediately and they, too, took me back to school early. I learned later from my mother that both mothers had told Mrs. French that I seemed sad and that was why they returned me ahead of schedule.

The couple who had sent over strawberries at the restaurant in London, Michael and Joanne Lyons, came to visit me one day and treat me to lunch at a rustic old inn in Sevenoaks. We had fresh rolls and butter that was molded into rosebuds. We had lamb chops with frilly paper on the bones and trifle for dessert. After lunch, we went for a walk in Sevenoaks and Mrs. Lyons held my hand. When she saw me staring at a doll wearing a Scottish kilt outfit in the window of a gift shop Mrs. Lyons asked, "Do you like that doll?"

"Oh, yes," I said. "She's beautiful!"

"Well, then, she's yours," and she gestured to the shopkeeper to take the doll out of the case. I fell in love with the Lyons. From that moment on, except for classes and activities, the doll was never out of sight. I loved her pretty face and her beautiful outfit, and she became a replacement for all the dolls I had had to give up when we left America.

When the Lyons brought me back to Farnaby, we took a leisurely walk on the school grounds and before they said good-by, they asked how I was doing at the school and was there anything I wanted them to tell my parents, any message to give them. My letters were censored, as the staff read everything before it was mailed. They sat right next to us as we wrote, looking over our shoulders to help, so there had been no way to tell my parents how desperately I missed them. I knew the Lyons were my only opportunity to let them know, and maybe if they had asked me before we got back to the school, I could have told them. I wanted to, and they sensed it.

"You can trust us," Mr. Lyons said. "We won't tell anyone except your parents what you said."

But there at the school, I was rooted to the spot, looking down at the ground and up at them, bursting with words that just wouldn't come. "Everything's all right," I said, even though nothing was and I ached for my parents all the time. Back in my dorm room I wondered why I hadn't asked the Lyons to get word of my plight to my parents and after that day I fretted constantly about not telling them.

That afternoon when the Lyons brought me back, just as every time I was returned to Farnaby, the last line from "'Twas the Night Before Christmas" echoed in my mind: "And I heard him exclaim, 'ere he drove out of sight, Merry Christmas to all and to all a good night." All the kind people who visited with me and took me out, then dropped me off at Farnaby and "drove out of sight," just as my parents had, never failed to reduce me to tears. I returned alone to my room, transported back to Christmases in Jackson Heights and all the times my parents had read the poem to me. I wept for my safe and secure past and all that I had lost.

Chapter 5

My Parents Arrive in Lagos

A couple of days after my parents left me at Farnaby, they departed London on a twin engine York bomber, with eighteen passengers and a crew of three. Flying all day, they crossed the English Channel, passing over Normandy, then down western France, within sight of the Pyrenees, and across the Mediterranean just as dusk set in. In the dark, the plane set down at the airport in Castel Benito, Tripoli, for a two-hour stopover for refueling and a change of crew from English to West African.

The passengers had time to eat dinner in the tiny restaurant and stroll about the airport, but there was no place to go or anything to see. Outside the airport it was pitch black, with a moonless sky studded by stars. The terminal was gloomy, lit only by a few bare twenty-watt bulbs hanging from black wire. My father relaxed in a leather armchair with a broken spring in front of a roaring fire, which was welcome in the chilly North African night.

It was the same chair with a broken spring that he had sat on when he made a stopover there a year earlier.

At ten that night, the plane took off for Kano, Nigeria, British West Africa, and it seemed to my parents that they had just fallen asleep when they were awakened by light streaming in the window from somewhere west of Suez. By seven o'clock, the big brassy sun was high and the desert floor was brightly lit. They were surprised to see that the sand below was reddish-brown, not white like the beaches around New York or the pictures of the Sahara they were familiar with.

As the plane closed in on Kano, they thought they could discern tiny figures moving about in compounds, and numerous paths that crisscrossed one another without seeming to go anywhere. Kano is one of the three walled cities mentioned in the Bible, and they were amazed to see below them ancient mud-walled towers, turrets, battlements, and minarets seemingly built in the best Hollywood tradition.

My parents were the only passengers to leave the plane in Kano. When they entered the airport four barefoot Nigerian customs officers in khaki shirts and shorts and red fezzes with black tassels surrounded them and smilingly murmured, "Welcome, sir." They asked for a "dash," pidgin-English for a tip or gift, but they gladly accepted a Chesterfield cigarette each. The head customs officer informed my parents that they needed to report to the police station for a permit to remain in Nigeria. There were no taxis or any kind of public transportation, so my father was in a quandary as to how to get there, and the grinning customs men offered no suggestions.

Just then an African trader my father had been corresponding with rushed up to greet them. Saleem Sabah, a Christian Arab, brushed aside the curious, clustering officials in the airport and drove my parents to the police station in his truck. In a one-room mud hut a mile outside the city of Kano, the British policeman/immigration officer examined their passports and visas. My father had no local currency, so Saleem Sabah advanced the ten-shilling fee the official demanded, and they were granted a fifteen-day permit. When my father protested that the British passport control office in New York had given him a one-year visa, and that he never would have taken a seven-thousand-mile trip for a mere two weeks, the policeman referred him to the immigration officer in Lagos, a thousand miles away, where they were headed the next day.

The policeman then buckled a gun belt around his waist and said casually that he had to investigate a ritual murder at a place called Nguru, and, climbing into his Land Rover, waved good-bye.

The thermometer in the shade near the entrance of the police station was registering one hundred twenty-one degrees. Saleem Sabbah was not impressed. He said it would go above one hundred thirty-five by midday. My parents, still dressed in the woolens they had been wearing in London the day before, were miserably hot. Saleem Sabbah drove them to a hotel in Kano where they bathed, rested, and changed into tropical clothes.

When they flew into Lagos on the seacoast the next

My parents in Lagos

day, they checked in at the Olympic, the only respectable hotel in town. The weather was extremely hot and sticky. The airline lost my father's briefcase with all of his important papers, including the letter of credit from his partners. Fortunately, his briefcase turned up at the airport after several anxiety-filled days, thoroughly rifled through, but with nothing essential missing.

Since my father had laid the groundwork before leaving New York, he was ready to begin trading as soon as his briefcase was found. A supplier from a distant part of the country came to see him at the hotel, and reported that there were from fifty to one hundred tons of galena ready to be bought at a good price. However, my father didn't have enough money to purchase more than ten tons. My mother was shocked that he would have come all the way to Africa with so little in the letter of credit.

Frantic cables and letters to his law firm partners in America advising that he needed more money right away went unanswered. He was confused by their lack of response, and afraid of being left without enough money to live on, as well as enough money to return to the United States. His grand business venture had ground to a halt before it even began. He cabled his brother Sidney to call the partners and tell them he was in a very risky situation and to find out why they hadn't responded and why the additional funds hadn't arrived.

Sidney, who was also a lawyer, wrote to my father that when he called him, the partner said, "I remitted funds via my bank yesterday. Lee should have received them by now."

"Are you sure about this?" Sidney asked. "I don't mean to offend you in any way. I only ask that question because my brother is in a precarious position and the money hasn't arrived yet."

When the line suddenly went dead Sidney called him right back. "Did you intend to hang up or were we cut off?"

"I had nothing else to say, and I don't want to talk to you any more," the partner replied.

"You certainly pick swell partners," Sidney wrote after his misadventure on the telephone. "I warned you at the time not to go ahead with the deal, but you were in such a rush to get off that you showed no sense at all.

While I'm willing to help you, I feel that you went into this with your eyes wide open and that if you have any ill effects, it's your own fault. From the very beginning, your partners struck me as heels and now I'm convinced they are, particularly since they can't even talk courteously on the telephone.

"Let me give you some brotherly advice: Watch out. Protect yourself. Don't let the proceeds of any sales get into your partners' hands. In view of their attitude and that screwed-up agreement that you worked out with them—which I didn't see until after you made it—I would like to be left entirely out of any negotiations with them."

My father, who had a younger brother's hunger for his older and more successful brother's approval, put the letter away, devastated by Sidney's sharp criticism.

Without the promised money to make purchases, my parents' emotions roller-coasted from confused to scared and back again. While my mother tossed and turned in bed at night, my father paced the halls of the Olympic. Each day brought deeper despair.

A week later the money from the partners finally arrived. My father's spirits soared as he made numerous calculations about what his income would be. He wrote to Sidney that if he could get one hundred tons of galena per month, he would have a monthly profit of $10,000. Even if he was being too optimistic and cut his projections in half, he would still rake in $5,000 per month on what he considered a very simple operation.

"Josie," he said to my mother as he planned his strategy, "now that I've received the money, I'm going to send my man, Animashaun, to Jos. There's a tin mine there I want him to check out. It'll take him three days by train. At the end of the line he'll go by truck for two hundred miles. After that he'll have to get a horse, somehow, and go twenty miles more to the galena deposit."

My mother asked, "Where's he going to get a truck and a horse in the middle of nowhere?"

"I don't know yet, but no vehicles can travel over the last twenty miles. They'll have to bring the tin to the road-side on donkeys. I guess I'll have to travel by horse, too, for the last part when I get up there. As soon as the ore gets rolling," he added, as if it had just occurred to him how difficult the process would be.

My father managed to find a car to rent while waiting for our Buick to arrive from America. It finally got there at the end of June, along with the rainy season. Now they had funding from the partners, their own transportation, and a welcome drop in temperature that made life more bearable.

Chapter 6

Letter to Hen

Lagos, Nigeria - May 1951
Dear Hen,
Well, here we are. It's like a dream. It can't be true that we really are in Nigeria, British West Africa. I have alternating states of excitement for an adventure and sheer panic at what we've done.

We're in a crummy hotel in Lagos (rhymes with Vegas), the capitol of Nigeria, and the city is teeming in a very primitive way. Since most places don't have indoor plumbing (although of course our hotel does), there are people whose job it is to collect "night soil," a very nice term for the excrement from people's toilets, called "thunder boxes." They collect it at night outside the house from a door in the thunder box and transport it in large bowls on their heads, and they're required to wear headlamps so that no one bumps into them in the dark.

Lee's business associate, Animashaun, is a Muslim with three wives. He is called Al Haji, which means he's been to Mecca, the holiest thing you can do as a Muslim.

We looked for the warmest school we could find in England for Alida. But my heart aches for her. She didn't seem to realize what was happening. She never questioned us and I think that she thought she was going to Africa with us. I'm not sure when we'll see her again and that's the hardest part for all of us. I'm sure she misses us and you and Helen and Jeannie terribly. She's been going to eight weeks of sleep-away camp since she was four, but that's not the same. I've been feeling very guilty and worried and hope she's all right.

As for me, I'm not sure what I'll do with all the time I'm going to have on my hands here with Lee working and nothing for me to do during the day and no place I could go alone. The American embassy people seem friendly enough, but I can't imagine I'm going to have any girlfriends and of course, I don't have you.

In a couple of weeks we plan to take a trip into the bush to view some locations for mines. Meanwhile, we're taking our malaria pills every day, and we're hoping to find a nicer place to live. We've gone to the club for drinks and socialization and I've noticed several men giving me the once-over.

Lagos is on the seacoast, so it's hot and steamy

and very "Casablanca." I've done a couple of paintings and we've been to the beach and the movies and we've gone dancing and it's kind of exotic.

Hope you and the kids are doing well. Write back soon—I could use the letters.

All my love,
Josie

Chapter 7

▼▼▼ ▼▼▼ ▼▼▼ ▼▼▼ ▼▼▼

Farnaby—Part II

My parents called me twice in the four or five months I was at Farnaby. The first time was two weeks after I had arrived, on my eighth birthday. I was playing a board game of Peter Rabbit that my parents had left with Mrs. French to give me as their present, when an older girl rushed up the stairs. Hurrying over to me she said breathlessly, "Your parents are calling from Africa!"

I ran down the main stairs, my heart pounding, and picked up the phone in the small dark hallway just outside the office. I knew Mrs. French was in there, on the other side of the closed door, listening.

"Hi, Dixiebelle," my father said. "Happy birthday! We miss you! How's school going?"

I tried hard to maintain control, but at the sound of his voice I started crying. "Daddy, why can't I be with you and Mommy?" I eked out between sobs. I could barely speak.

50

"We'll send for you as soon as we can," he answered. "The hotel we're staying at is no place for a little girl. There's no school in Lagos and nothing for you to do. You'd be very bored and unhappy."

"But, Daddy, I miss you so much. Please, please let me come. I promise I'll be good."

"Alida," my father said, "it's not a matter of being good. You didn't do anything wrong. It's just that there's no school here for you. As soon as school vacation starts, I promise, we'll bring you here."

How could my parents have heard me and not come for me? I was their only child—how could they have left me in England as casually as my mother had left her leopard coat in storage?

Everyone at school missed their parents, but at least the other girls knew they would see them again. Their parents visited, they went home for vacations and occasional weekends. At night before I fell asleep I would try to conjure up the image of my parents' faces. I would lie there in the dark after everyone had said good night and try to recall the way they looked and sounded, but it got more difficult with time. Eventually I gave up hope that we would ever be together again.

I missed all the familiar things and people in my life— not only my parents, but my dear cousins, Helen and Jeannie, their mother, Hen, and my two best friends, Helen and Susan. I couldn't talk to anyone who had known me before Farnaby.

I missed Susan and Helen. We had all gotten the same baby dolls. They were life-size and had eyes that opened and closed as well as moved side to side, so people would think we were holding real babies and look askance at us and our mothers.

I used to have sleepovers with Jeannie and we would giggle late into the night. When my mother came in to check up on us, we would feign sleep, but we could never fool her.

I missed my cats, Topsy and Dinah. We had a tall antique cabinet that the cats could jump to from the dining table. My father used to poke a piece of paper up through the slats at the top of the cabinet, and we would laugh at their antics as they tried to catch the paper.

I missed my beautiful bedroom. My mother, a talented artist, had painted my headboard and dresser bottle-green and spray-painted the sisal rug white and hand-painted it with flowers. She had sewn the bedspread in green chintz to match the headboard, with white eyelet lace trim, and painstakingly threaded it with yellow grosgrain ribbon. She made a white smocked skirt for my dressing table and lampshades out of two layers of clear plastic into which she inserted dried flowers and stitched the layers together.

I used to walk down the block alone to the corner candy store to buy the *Herald Tribune* on Sunday mornings so that I could follow along with the Comic Weekly Man as he read the comics on the radio. I had left behind my favorite comic books—*Little Lulu, Archie, Sheena Queen of the Jungle, Donald Duck, Nancy*—and radio programs that I would listen to on car trips or in my bedroom on an enormous radio, so big it stood on the floor and was almost as tall as I was. "The Great Gildersleeve," "Henry

Aldrich," "The Shadow." These had been part of the fabric of my life.

We got my Uncle Dan's used television in 1949 and I loved to watch Howdy Doody, Captain Video, The Lone Ranger, Gene Autry, and Gary Moore and his sidekick, Durwood Kirby, so much that I liked getting sick, or pretending I was, so I could stay home from school to see the shows. There was no radio or television at Farnaby, no curling up on a cozy sofa and watching my favorite programs.

We had a large pre-war apartment in Jackson Heights, with two bedrooms and two bathrooms in a garden apartment that encircled a large area where we could safely ride our bicycles. My friends and I would build leaf houses in the fall and capture fireflies in bottles on a summer evening. I went to school, the circus, movies, and restaurants. There were trips to New York City. This was my life, and as far as I was concerned, it was just fine. It didn't need to change—or vanish completely.

There was one thing I saved for when things got really tough—the whistle that my family used if we got separated when we were out and were looking for each other. It had three notes. My father said each note was for a syllable in my mother's name. "Jo-se-phine," we would whistle. When I was really desperate for my parents at Farnaby, I could whistle her name and while it caused a stab of pain in my stomach and aching in my heart, it helped me feel an almost tangible connection with them. I could "reach" them by making the exact same sound that they made and I saved it for really bad moments.

There was a swimming pool through the woods on the school grounds. Swimming was required even though the air was cool. The pool was unheated and there were always dead leaves floating in it. We had to go in and the swim instructor, who was standing alongside the pool, wouldn't let us out until we had begged and begged.

"No," she would say, "your lips aren't purple yet."

I wasn't a swimmer and I would hang onto the side of the pool, shivering and praying to get out. My mother would have made them let me out. She wouldn't have wanted me to be cold. She might have even told them not to make me swim at all.

One afternoon, walking back alone from the pool, I heard a faint voice. It was my mother calling my name. "Ali..i..i..da." Startled, I stopped and looked around for her, but she wasn't there. No one was. I was all alone in the woods, with only the bluebells, the trees, and the birds.

Another day, just before bedtime, a teacher who boarded at the school came into my dorm room. She was shocked to see how chapped and sore my hands were.

"I'll be right back," she said. She went to her room and got a jar of Nivea cream and gently rubbed it into my skin. Then she brushed my hair and wanted to put it back in a ponytail.

I shook my head. "No, my mother said I should never wear my hair back because my ears stick out."

"What a thing to tell a child," she muttered under her breath, letting my hair fall back into place.

Spring vacation came and the school cleared out, except for some girls who couldn't go home for various reasons. The few staff who remained loosened up and let us participate in activities with them. They taught us songs like "La Plume de Ma Tante," "Alive-Alive-o," and "Sur le Pont d'Avignon" and we helped them wallpaper a small bedroom. "Dab-in-it here, dab-in-it there," we sang and laughed as we got wallpaper paste on our hands, clothes, and hair.

Summer vacation arrived and the entire student body went home with the exception of Beatrice, whose mother was very sick, and me, despite the fact that my father had said I would join them when school let out. We were joined by two other children from a nearby boys' school. Albert was only six years old, the son of an African mother and a white father who lived in the Gold Coast. He had seen his parents, briefly, only two times in the past three years. That made him worse off than I was.

Prince Omar, who was eight, was a nephew of King Farouk of Egypt. The two boys must have been in England a long time, because they both had perfect British accents. The four of us were together all day, every day, the best of friends. One time a bench in the dining room where we were raucously playing fell over on Albert's leg. When he cried, Omar said, "Buck up, old chap," to console him and let him know we all felt bad for him.

Three brown Shetland ponies grazed in a field near Farnaby, and we would walk there to pet them and feed them apples. I loved those shaggy little ponies, as they were my size and very gentle, and seemed glad to have our company.

Cook gave us money and rationing coupons for

candy and we skipped into the town of Sevenoaks and bought chocolate bars. We were free to come and go as we pleased. There didn't seem to be any supervision, nor, in my memory, any one else except for Cook and her cat.

When we awoke one morning we were shocked to see snow on the ground.

"It's Christmas!" Omar said.

"It's Christmas!" we echoed, dancing around. It was July, but we were only eight years old and we were excited, believing it really was Christmas. The snow lasted only a few hours before the warm summer sun rose in the sky and melted it.

Chapter 8

Life in Lagos

Dear Sidney," my father wrote. "We spoke to Alida, and despite your and Mom's disapproval, she likes Farnaby very much and hopes she can stay there for the next term. She seems to be picking up a lot of polish from the Brits. We're pretty well satisfied that she's in a good school and is happy and that it's a very good experience for her."

Though he had no evidence at that point of my academic standing relative to my peers in America, in order to dispel Sidney's concern about me my father bragged that I was well ahead of my grade in school, so nothing was lost. He added that they were planning to keep me at Farnaby for the next semester, which would start in September. If they had enough money. He knew from our phone call that I was miserable. Nevertheless he ticked off some of the things I had written about in my censored letters, penned with one of the staff standing over me. "She's been to London for the weekend with friends of ours and taken a trip down the Thames. She takes horseback riding and she's learning French."

My parents were still in the Olympic Hotel, which my father said wasn't satisfactory for a child and it seemed there were no houses to rent, although he said they had tried to find one. He wrote to Sidney that when the school term ended, either I would join them in Lagos for the holidays or my mother would go to England and take "the kid," as he called me, to Europe, provided he was getting and shipping the galena and making the contemplated profits. School had ended about six weeks before, but I remained there. And I wonder—when they decided not to have me join them when summer vacation began and all the other girls went home, did they know Beatrice would be there with me? Did they know that Prince Omar and Albert would join us? Would they have left me at Farnaby even if there had been no other children?

When the expected profits didn't materialize, my parents decided I should join them in Lagos. Just in time for my arrival, they succeeded in renting a house in the best European section. My father wrote to Sidney that they were counting the minutes until I arrived. He added that he was still debating whether to keep me with them or send me back to England when the new school term started.

They were meeting a lot of people and my father was trying to cultivate government officials for help with his business. Because he was one of the few Americans in Lagos who wasn't either a missionary or an employee of the American consulate, he was considered an interesting newcomer, and my parents received many social invitations. They attended a cocktail party at the American vice consul's house to meet the new consul general, and then they were invited by the consul general to a July Fourth celebration, where he won a little money playing poker and made some friends.

The next night they visited a seedy African nightclub with the Greek captain of the ship that had brought their car from America. That's the way it was there. All the white people befriended one another and socialized because there were so few of them and precious few white women. They were enjoying a cigarette and a Scotch when the band began to play "Smoke Gets in Your Eyes."

"Dance with your beautiful girl," the captain murmured sadly. "I didn't dance with mine and someone stole her from me."

Almost from day one my father and mother disagreed about Nigeria. Over dinner at the Olympic he said, "You can make a lot of dough here, if you know how, and I think it's an interesting place."

My mother replied, "Maybe you *can* make a lot of money here. But for me it's dull and uncomfortable, and no place to be except on business. There's nowhere to take a ride to except the beach and how many times can you go there? Even the movies are old and lousy—twenty years old and down to the unsophisticated African level. And there's nothing for me to do all day!"

As little as my mother had to occupy her time, my father had too much to do. Especially in the beginning, it was a tug-of-war to get the products my father wanted to purchase because the suppliers in the bush were afraid to bring their merchandise down to Lagos. They worried that when they got there my father might change his mind and not take the goods at all or offer them less money than they had agreed upon in their correspondence. However, once some of them tried it, they found that they were paid cash out of his over-the-shoulder airline bag as soon as the weighing was completed. Word spread upcountry, and deliveries began to increase.

On a particularly hot and humid morning in July, my father was up and dressed by five. Too excited to eat, he left the hotel without waking my mother. This was the day he had been waiting for since his arrival in Nigeria. He was going to load his first shipment to the States—fifty tons of cow bones, which he said "stank to high heaven," five tons of kola nuts, and one ton of ginger. He threaded his car through the narrow streets of Lagos, anxious to be there before the truckers and the ship arrived. Even at that hour, the docks were bustling. The air was heavy with impending rain, the gray sky was misty, and the ship was nowhere in sight.

He found the truckers who had brought his shipment from upcountry, but decided not to unload the trucks until the ship was in the harbor. As the hours passed, he grew restless and hungry.

Finally, around noon, the ship appeared out of the fog, but the barge he needed to bring the bones, kola nuts, and ginger from the dock to the ship had departed an hour earlier for its next scheduled job. When it returned to carry my father's shipment it went to the wrong wharf. He finally got it redirected to his wharf, but the crew failed to tie it to the pier. That caused a commotion among the truck drivers when they saw the barge float away on the changing tide.

It took another hour to get the barge back to my father's wharf. As the barefoot truckers and dockworkers began to unload the goods from the trucks, a bag filled with bones broke. Then several bags of kola nuts broke. The head trucker went to my father. "Sah," he said, "my men must have more money. Too many hours waiting." Then he demanded, "Many bags broken, sah. More money to sew or change."

My father's head began to pound, but with no choice, he agreed to the demands. As unloading the trucks and repairing the bags and re-loading onto the barge was under way, the sky opened up and the rain that had been threatening all day began to pour down, drenching the shipment, my father, and all the workers. By the time the bones, kola nuts, and ginger were on their way to America, it was dark and the end of one of the most exciting and stressful days of my father's life. What he had expected would be the easiest of tasks, shipping the goods he had already gathered, had proven to be much more complex than he ever imagined.

In the following days he waited anxiously for a freight car with galena from his supplier upcountry to arrive in Lagos in time to meet the next ship. He needed 150 tons and only had 64. His life became hectic as he bought more goods, worried about their timely arrival, got them on ships, and found buyers. He hadn't relaxed once since they arrived in Nigeria, and he wrote to Sidney that he thought he was headed for ulcers.

"We're at the point where we barely have enough money for a month's living expenses and our emergency fund for return fare," he wrote to Sidney. How he longed to be able to tell his partners to go to hell, both for what they were doing to him and for hanging up on Sidney. He began to supplement his income by buying more cow bones. He decided he could get more bones if he went in person into the bush.

They left early on a Friday morning—my father, my mother, and Animashaun. My father wore tan bush shorts,

On the back of this photo my father wrote,
"Isn't she a beauty?"

a tan shirt and his sun helmet. Even though they were going into the bush, my mother wore an outfit nice enough to wear to a tea party—a light green dress, dark green hat, a purse, and matching low heels. Animashaun was portly and dignified with his African robes hanging loosely over his stomach.

They arrived at their first destination, a small village with forty round mud huts and pointed thatched roofs, and were greeted by people running out of their houses waving and clapping. They held up their right arms with hand closed, in friendship, to show they were holding no weapons. They seemed immensely pleased when my father returned the sign, indicating that he, too, had only peaceful and friendly intentions.

As he negotiated with the chief for bones, their car was besieged by a mob that had never seen anything like a Buick convertible. They formed a circle around the car and were amazed when my father made the roof and the windows go up and down with the push of a button. They pointed to the radio antenna and gawked at the dashboard. Adults smiled and children laughed and jumped around; they seemed excited about having such amazing visitors. My father concluded a deal to purchase the bones.

Before they left, my parents attended a juju ceremony. About forty people had been waiting for the witch doctor. When he arrived, he walked into the middle of the circle they had formed. After some chanting, he pulled a live chicken from a basket. As he held the chicken by its neck, it struggled to get away, clucking and scattering feathers, but the witch doctor lifted it up to the sky and without hesitation, drew a knife across its neck. Blood squirted from the chicken and covered the witch doctor and spattered on the ground.

My mother screamed and everyone turned to look at her. Her scream broke the spell and disrupted the ceremony. People muttered to each other and began to leave. The witch doctor scowled ominously and loudly cursed my parents, who edged their way cautiously back to the car. They got in as quickly as possible, and drove off, with the witch doctor running behind them, yelling and shaking his fist.

At a smaller village about ten miles away, after the palaver about the purchase of more bones was over, my mother bought a native robe with intricate embroidery from the emir's son. It was white cotton with a thin blue stripe and the embroidery was sewn in gold-colored thread. My father put it on and dozens of people crowded around to see him wearing it. When my father took out his camera and pointed it at the Africans, the whole group began to run away, fearful the camera would steal their soul.

A few miles from that village, the road petered out at an almost dry riverbed. They debated what to do and my father decided to cross it, but the car became trapped on the loose rocks at the bottom of the river and couldn't get the traction it needed to continue across. The wheels spun and dug in but still the car wouldn't move.

As they were worriedly pondering what to do, out of the seemingly empty landscape a few men appeared. Six of them pushed on the car, accompanied by a series of chanting grunts that sounded like, "Ah hah, ah hee, ah hah, ah hee." It took a while to get some forward motion, but eventually the car began to move. Several other Africans watched and cheered as it finally reached the other side. They seemed pleased when my father gave each man two cigarettes in thanks for their help.

My father was elated and relieved that he had been successful in making the purchases and they returned to Lagos on Monday night. They had slept at two primitive government rest stations along the way, and driven five hundred and seventy miles on rutted, bumpy dirt roads.

By the time they got back to Lagos my mother had developed fever and chills. When it was diagnosed as malaria, she had to go into the hospital. Even though she felt really sick, the doctor said she just had a slight touch of it and would only be there for two or three days. Unfortunately, with malaria, no immunity is acquired from having it.

"Dear Sidney," my father wrote. "We've just returned from a successful trip in the bush to purchase cow bones. Jo got malaria, but I was able to get five tons of bones and will make a profit of thirty dollars per ton. I know that's not a lot, but it will help tide us over until the real money starts rolling in."

Chapter 9

❖❖❖❖❖

Father O'Sullivan and the Andrews Sisters

My parents had been in Lagos a couple of months when my father made arrangements to fly to Ishiago to purchase galena from an emir who owned some mines. To save money, Animashaun left three days ahead of him to go by coastal steamer to Port Harcourt, about eighty miles from the mines.

My father booked a seat on West African Airways, which operated a small single-engine plane for a trip that would take four or five hours. There was a one-hour stopover at a bush airport, where they were served tea. Drinking hard liquor in the middle of the day was contrary to the unwritten rule of Africa never to drink before sundown. Nevertheless, one of the passengers, an Englishwoman who was obviously an "old coaster," took her refreshment from a whiskey flask.

Animashaun greeted my father at the airport outside

of Port Harcourt in a small, shabby truck he had rented
and drove him to the government catering rest house. He
was assigned to share a chalet with an Englishman who
represented the British-American Tobacco Company. Animashaun was given a small room in the back where the
workers stayed. The steward told my father he could only
have his room for three days, and my father assured him
he would be out by that time. He planned to be back in
Lagos within three days with all the galena he needed.

How wrong he would be.

The next morning, he and Animashaun went to the
marketplace to buy bags for the ore. The market was
teeming with activity from all the vendors who had set
up stalls and tents and tables to display their wares. When
they found a seller for the bags, my father was asked to
pay what he was sure was double the going price. Animashaun suggested that the reason for the high quote was
my father's white skin and said that if he waited out of
sight, Animashaun could buy bags at the market price. So
much for white skin being an advantage as my father had
thought it would be back in America. When the transac-
tion was completed, they were anxious to be off to Ishiago, but the car Animashaun had arranged for didn't arrive
until the next morning.

The steward who was serving my father breakfast before his departure expressed alarm at his plan to go into
Ishiago territory, warning that cannibals lived there. As
my father ate his breakfast, the steward told him that the
cannibals considered the cheeks, the ball of the fingers

and the heel of the palm as special delicacies, but that they liked to "chop," or eat, any part of the body. Having heard this kind of talk whenever he mentioned going into the bush, my father paid no attention. He attributed the chatter to a conspiracy to keep him from competing with the native traders, who claimed that only they could go into the interior, where no white man could go and come out alive. If they weren't invoking cannibals to scare him away, it was snakes, scorpions, leopards, tsetse flies, or hostile natives.

After breakfast he went back to his chalet to get his little over-the-shoulder airline bag. Into it he put a whiskey bottle filled with water, a box of tissues, a Boy Scout knife, a tin of Band-Aids, a carton of cigarettes, a tube of Aureomycin and a wad of cash, as well as the sandwiches the cook at the rest house had made for him. In the photo that he had his English roommate take that day, he is wearing a white drill bush jacket, shorts, a surplus U.S. Army sun helmet and ankle-high desert boots and is carrying a machete.

"I'm off to Ishiago," he said casually to the roommate. "I'll be back tonight." The other man raised his eyebrows but only said politely, "Good luck, old boy."

They left the rest house at ten that morning. Besides my father and Animashaun, there was the driver, Jacob; a young native named Mbulu, who said he knew how to trade with the tribe from whom they would be purchasing the ore; and Nathan Nwokye. Nwokye was the trader who had sent the galena sample to my father in New York. He kept trying to convince my father to give him the money to purchase the galena and that he should go alone. Because Nwokye was an Ibo and Animashaun was Hausa, Animashaun thought he should not be trusted with my father's money. However, he thought that they ought to take Nwokye with them because he had bought galena in that area before and might be useful.

At first the road to Ishiago was surprisingly smooth. For the first ten miles or so it was tarred, or "metalled," as the British say. From then on it was hard, bumpy laterite, a reddish clay-like material. At noon, about fifty miles out of Port Harcourt, they decided to take a lunch break in Aba, a sprawling village of about a thousand people. It was market day and the population had swelled to triple that number because of all the people who had come from the surrounding area to sell their produce and to make purchases.

My father's party parked near the market and his travel companions left to buy their lunch. A crowd of curious Africans collected around his car, forming a circle about ten feet away, staring silently while he ate his sandwiches. They scurried away when he took out his camera and pointed it at them, but gradually they became emboldened and surrounded the car again.

The people in his party drifted back in half an hour, all except the driver, Jacob, who didn't turn up until an hour later, as my father was beginning to fret about getting up and back before nighttime. To my father's consternation, Jacob said that he had telephoned his master and had instructions not to go to Ishiago but to return to Port Harcourt right away. He was adamant about not continuing the trip. He said that people in town had warned him that if he went to Ishiago the natives there would break his car and "chop" him. He ignored promises of extra money as well as threats.

Just as my father was beginning to despair about being able to complete his journey, an African policeman rode up on a bicycle. My father hailed him and he dismounted, clicked his heels, and saluted. My father asked him to take them all to the police station where they found a hard-boiled British officer in charge and they told him what was happening.

The officer informed my father that there were, in fact, cannibals in Ishiago, but, he said authoritatively, "The British have put the fear of God into them and they would not dare molest a white man, so you will be quite safe. As for your men," he warned, "those from a different part of the country are safe so long as they stay near you, and don't drift off into the bush or wander around at night. If they disappear the police will be powerless to do anything about it."

My father asked him to assure Jacob that he was in no danger. "I'll try," he replied, "But it will probably do no good—your man is obviously thoroughly frightened and set on returning."

Turning to Jacob, he asked who had told him that his car would be broken and he would be chopped. Jacob, with great hesitancy, said, "Nwokye." As he did so, the latter sneered visibly. In the middle of the sneer, the policeman slapped Nwokye across the face. In a twinkling, he changed from a haughty Ibo into a groveling servant, mumbling, "Please master, please master, please master."

The policeman growled at him, "Now tell the driver that no one will break his car or chop him and that he will be safe with master. Mind you, no hanky-panky in your own language to him." Nwokye, thoroughly cowed, did as he was told. Though he was obviously still nervous, Jacob agreed to proceed with the trip.

Animashaun, who had watched the proceedings without moving a muscle in his face, now said, "Let's go, sah. We have lost too much time already." When they got back into the car, Nwokye started to get in. My father pulled him out and declared, "You're finished. I don't want to have anything more to do with you! You're a traitor who's tried to spoil my whole trip."

Nwokye groveled on the ground and, then to my father's disgust, kissed his shoes. Finally, Animashaun whispered that perhaps they ought to let him come as he might be useful, and besides, he would watch Nwokye closely.

My father asked Nwokye, "How do I know I can trust you?"

Nwokye replied, "I swear by juju that I will be faithful. If I am not, juju will strike me dead."

My father answered, "I don't know what juju will do to you, but I know what I'll do. I'll strangle you if you try any more hanky-panky." Then, as time was wasting, he relented and let him into the car.

The road went through dense jungle and over dry watercourses and though it narrowed to a track at times, it remained fairly passable. After several hours they arrived at a station on the Nigerian Railway called Afikpo Road, which Animashaun said was about five miles from Ishia-go. He asked my father to wait for them at the Afikpo sta-tion while he and the others went on to Ishiago because, if the natives knew that a white man wanted to buy, they would double their price. My father trusted Animashaun, so he gave him all his cash along with final instructions about the highest price to pay.

As Animashaun and the others disappeared in the car toward Ishiago, he settled down under a small open shed on the station platform, out of the burning sun. The tem-perature was at least one hundred twenty degrees, since it was only a couple of hundred miles north of the Equator in the dry season, the hottest time of the year. With no one around and nothing to do, he drowsed. He awoke to see a bicyclist with a sun helmet come down one of the paths out of the bush toward the station. Under the helmet was a young white man who called out in a rollicking Irish brogue, "And what might you be doing, passing the time of day at this out-of-the-way place? I'm Father O'Sulli-van of Dublin," he continued. "I conduct a mission near Ishiago."

My father introduced himself and explained that the men he had come with had taken his car to Ishiago and should be back soon.

"Where are you expecting to spend the night?" the priest asked.

It was nearing four o'clock and my father now real-ized there was no chance of getting back to Port Harcourt that day.

"The nearest catering rest house is at Onitsha, over

sixty miles away. You'll never get there tonight because of the poor roads. You're welcome to stay at my place," Father O'Sullivan said, and he pointed in the direction where the car had gone.

My father gratefully accepted the priest's invitation.

"My house is about three miles from here. If your people have started back, I'll meet them on the road and tell them where you are. Cheerio!" With that, Father O'Sullivan left.

My father waited another hour but there was no sign of his men. It would be dark in two more hours, so he decided to walk to the mission and started down the road. Daylight was ending, but it was still cruelly hot and the road was dusty. He hadn't walked three miles since he was a Boy Scout, age twelve, a long time before. As his clothes grew wet, the dust caked on his body and the little overnight bag grew heavy. He walked on and as he walked, tall, naked men, wearing palm thatches on their heads and carrying machetes, appeared out of the bush alongside the road and walked beside, behind and in front of him. As each man approached, he raised his thatch and murmured, "Good evening, Father."

Eventually, there were about thirty of them. They seemed unthreatening but how was one to know? "My God," he thought, "I've certainly come a long way from Wall Street. Who would believe this!" He was becoming more and more nervous but, after walking silently alongside him for a while, without a word, the men began to drift off into the bush again.

He was pretty sure that he was on the right road, because it seemed to be the only road and Father O'Sullivan had said it was, but he was feeling more lost and forlorn and vulnerable with each step he took. He worried about how he would find his way to the priest's house if he didn't arrive before dark. He wondered what kind of wild animals might be out there or whether he would encounter unfriendly natives. His walk to Father O'Sullivan's house was beginning to give new meaning to the word "alone." He had finished his sandwiches and water hours before. He asked himself why Animashaun hadn't come back for him. How long could the negotiations possibly take? Why would his men leave him at the station for such a long time and not come to inquire about his well-being or inform him of what was happening, since the mines were only five miles from Afikpo Road station? Why had he given Animashaun all his money? He reflected that he certainly had put himself in a precarious position, unarmed and with no money or car.

As he came to a bend in the road, he saw a native mud hut surrounded by a cactus palisade, its grass roof sticking above the wall. He thought he heard music, and as he came closer and listened, to his amazement, my father realized that what he was hearing was a record he had owned at home, none other than the Andrews Sisters' "Yodelin' Jive." He would never know how the occupants of that hut came by the hand-winder or that record, but he did know that it certainly was incongruous. He wanted to peek into the hut to see who was playing the record, but was afraid of a hostile reaction. No doubt about it: this was something to write home about.

My father was exhausted but determined to reach Father O'Sullivan's house before dark. The road seemed never-ending, and the potential dangers became magnified as he imagined the worst. He pictured himself disappearing from the face of the earth, due to either man or animal, and neither Animashaun nor my mother ever knowing what had happened to him.

Finally, to his enormous relief, he reached his destination just as Father O'Sullivan was about to depart to a small village for evening prayers. He said he would be back shortly, and asked if my father would like to take a shower. Showers in West Africa were for the servants of Europeans; the white man used a bathtub. My father had often envied his servants in Lagos, but they stuck to their quarters and their shower, and he stuck to his quarters and his bathtub.

My father said in disbelief, "Are you pulling my leg?"

"Not atall, atall," the priest answered. " 'Tis a proper bush shower. Come, I'll show you how it works. You pull this string hanging from the bucket and the water comes through the holes in the bottom. To stop it, you pull the string again. My boy will show you your bedroom and give you soap and a towel. Make yourself comfortable until I come back. Cheerio!"

My father hastened to take off his sweaty clothes and went to the shower, which was in a little alcove outside the back of the house. He pulled the string and, just as Father O'Sullivan had told him, the water came out like a proper shower. He soaped up and—much to his consternation— there was no more water! He wasn't dirty anymore, but he was very soapy. Frustrated, he yanked the string again and again in the vain hope that there would be water.

It grew dark with a suddenness as if someone had drawn a black curtain across the sky. The soap began to dry on his body and he was very uncomfortable. Though he heard mosquitoes buzzing around, he got not a single bite, probably due to the soap. He yelled for Abraham, Father O'Sullivan's steward, but echoes from the darkness around him were the only response. There were no lights visible in the house and he could never have found his way in the dark; besides, going back to his room would scarcely have improved his situation.

He couldn't tell how long he stood in the darkness shouting for Abraham. It might have been five minutes but it felt like half an hour, when the steward came trotting up with a kerosene hurricane lantern. He explained that he had been preparing chop for the masters in the kitchen on the other side of the house and had heard my father calling but needed to attend to his cooking before he could help. He lifted the bucket off its hook on the ceiling, took it away and soon came back with a full one. It was a little muddy, but it served the purpose and my father was able to rinse the soap off.

His sweaty clothing was drying rapidly. While waiting for Father O'Sullivan to return, my father sat in the living room with the towel around him and read an old *Saturday Evening Post*. Upon the priest's return, my father got dressed and they had dinner. The priest explained that the men my father had met along the road were farmers and that the only white men they had ever seen were missionary priests, and that was why they had addressed him as "Father."

They chatted amiably and Father O'Sullivan tactfully refrained from asking what had landed my father in such an isolated place. My father soon volunteered that he was headed to Ishiago to buy galena for export and the priest gave him helpful suggestions about the local customs so that he wouldn't violate any taboos. The priest then sent Abraham to tell my father's party that he was at Father O'Sullivan's house and Animashaun sent back word that they would join him later.

When my father's men came to the house about nine that night, Animashaun reported that they had not bought anything yet, but that progress was satisfactory. He said that, though he was not allowed to see the place where the ore was mined, he had seen heaps of it in various huts and understood that an ample supply would be available; it was only a question of price. My father emphasized to him the importance not only of making a purchase on this trip, but of making an arrangement for steady supplies in the future. Animashaun pointed out that that was the reason they must not be hasty, and the others agreed.

My father swallowed an anti-malaria pill and crawled under his mosquito netting for the night.

Chapter 10

▼ ▼ ▼ ▼ ▼

The Cannibals

The next day my father awoke to find that Animashaun and the others had already left for Ishiago. By noon Nwoke and Animashaun returned to report that an agreement had been reached.

"Sah," Animashaun said, "The chief has all the ore you need. He wants to sell it by the heap."

"How much do you estimate the heap weighs?" my father asked.

"Over five tons, sah."

The amount the chief was asking was within the price limit. Animashaun asked my father's approval of the deal, but, my father said, "You have to buy by the ton, not by a 'heap.'"

Animashaun said, "That is how the people here trade, sah." My father was adamant. He wouldn't buy unless he knew the weight.

"The time has come for me to talk with the chief my-self. Just because he wants a higher price from a white man doesn't mean that he'll get it."

As Jacob, Nwoke, Animashaun, and my father drove into the village, children scurried out of sight. There were no women visible, only men wearing little or no clothes. When they got out of the car my father said to Animashaun, "I don't believe these people are cannibals. It's just a story to keep strangers away."

Animashaun said, "Do you see that little house there, sah?" It looked like a corn crib, full of chicken feathers. "That is a juju house. Poke your machete into the feathers."

My father put his machete into the feathers. He un-covered one skull and another and then was horrified to see numerous human skulls nestled there. The hair on his arms rose and he shivered involuntarily as he jumped back. "I'm going to finish my business," he said to him-self, "and get out of here, pronto."

They came to the largest hut, where the chief, in an orange sarong, and about ten of his men, prostrated them-selves before my father as a mark of respect. My father told Animashaun to ask them to stand up. Everyone but the chief was completely naked. They all went into the hut where the chief showed him a heap of ore in the corner, which my father saw at a glance was excellent quality. He asked where the five tons were and was told that this was it. It was preposterous, but he refrained from saying so out loud, because even though the cannibals didn't un-derstand English, the treacherous Nwokye might translate what he said. Instead, he asked Animashaun to weigh the heap on the scale he had brought with him. It was less than one ton.

Then the negotiations began. "These people are much better traders than they appear—no wonder they want to sell by the heap," my father remarked to Animashaun. He wanted to tell the chief to stuff it, but he noticed a very large pot into which he could have fit. He remembered the skulls and decided to hold his tongue.

The trading went on and on and became very animated. Here and there he detected what sounded like an English word. He ventured to Animashaun, "I thought you didn't know the local language."

Animashaun laughed and said, "I don't. Don't you know what we are talking, sah? It is this rotten English which you call pidgin."

They were getting nowhere. My father's men complained that they were thirsty and the cannibals wouldn't give them any water.

"The hell with these savages," my father said quietly to Animashaun. "Let's go. Tell them I will be at Father O'Sullivan's house. Tell them our best price and if they change their minds I'll be there tonight and they can send word. I'm leaving tomorrow. When they find that no one will pay their ridiculous price, and they're ready to come down to earth, they can tell the Father. He promised to send word to Mbulu in Port Harcourt and Mbulu will send me a telegram. That's my last word."

As he turned to go he decided to take a snapshot of the chief. As soon as he became aware that my father was focusing the camera in his direction, the chief fled among the trees and then timorously peeked out from behind a big trunk.

"The chief probably thinks the camera is a firearm, sah. Better put it away," Animashaun urged.

When they arrived back at the mission, Father O'Sullivan greeted them and said, "I'd be grateful if you would drive me to a town that's about fifteen miles away. I have some shopping to do and I want to see the priests at the mission. I haven't seen them for several months."

My father was happy to do what he could to repay his host's hospitality. Since Father O'Sullivan was refusing any payment, when they got to the town, he bought him several bottles of wine and a carton of cigarettes, which the priest said he had run out of.

When they went to the big mission, the three priests there seemed happy to see a new face and shook my father's hand warmly. Irishmen all, they served him a quart bottle of cold beer, and merrily asked, "How are the Brooklyn Dodgers making out? And what do you think of the Notre Dame football team?

"There's scarcely a family in Ireland that doesn't have one or more relatives in America. We know as much about America as we know about Ireland," they boasted.

There were some sly digs at the British. They were so much warmer and more animated than the British that he felt he was among friends for the first time since he had come to Africa.

The next morning he said good-bye to the Priest of the Bush and my father and his party left. When he got back to the rest house at Port Harcourt he went straight to his chalet. It was now occupied by the British-American Tobacco man and another man, who were both quite surprised and relieved to see him.

"When you didn't return the first night and the next one, I reported your absence to the District Officer. He decided to wait one more day before sending out a search party. You were in very bad country. I really regretted not trying to dissuade you from going there," the tobacco man said.

My father pooh-poohed his concerns but the roommate protested that a number of people had disappeared in that area. Their disappearance had been hushed up because there was nothing the police were able to do about it. My father informed the District Officer that he had returned and the D.O. sternly told him that he had put himself in a position of considerable jeopardy by naïvely going into that territory alone and unarmed.

He was anxious to get back to Lagos, knowing that my mother had been expecting him back three days earlier and would be worried. He contacted the airline office and learned that a plane was scheduled to leave for Lagos at noon the next day, but that it was filled. He made numerous frustrating calls to the airline, which insisted that there were no openings. "You might take a chance and go to the airport just in case someone who was booked doesn't show up," the booking agent finally suggested.

My father arranged for transportation to the airport and anxiously watched the plane come in from the Cameroons. No one got off except the two-man crew. There was one other passenger waiting to go on board, a young Englishman who had served a two-year tour in West Africa. When they boarded the plane they turned out to be the only two passengers.

The trip back to Lagos was scary. The plane continually hit air pockets and seemed to drop hundreds of feet, only to climb again. Sometimes the jungle and mangrove swamps seemed very close. Below, everything looked matted, dense, and bright green. They followed the coastline and now and then flew over the ocean.

"It's hard to believe," my father mused, "but I used to swim at Jones Beach on the other side of this same ocean."

During the flight he had time to reflect on his trip into the bush. He had come a long way, paid a considerable sum of money, and risked his life, to no avail. The cannibal seemed set on doing business his way, and my father had been unable to purchase any galena or make arrangements for future purchases. He had failed and was coming back to Lagos empty-handed.

Several times the pilot opened the door to his cabin, looked around at them and smiled. The other passenger was a cold fish who scarcely uttered a word. He implied that, having been in Africa for two years and now headed for home, he didn't want to speak about it and would like nothing better than to forget everything. However, it turned out that my father was fortunate to be on the same plane with his close-mouthed companion since there was no ground transportation when they arrived at the airport in Lagos. When the other man was met by his company station wagon, the driver agreed to take my father to his hotel.

He arrived at the Olympic Hotel just as tea was being served. As he walked into their room, my mother greeted him with a casual, "Hi."

"You act as if you were expecting me, so you must have received my telegram," he answered.

"No, I didn't get your telegram," she replied. "It'll probably come in a day or two. But I knew you were coming."

"How did you know that, when I didn't know it myself, until four hours ago, at noontime?"

"Oh, that was easy. You know those African chums who are always coming around, knocking at the door, to sell kola nuts, ginger, rubber, and the other what-all you buy? Well, the day you left, they stopped coming; not one of them was here while you were gone. But today, they started to come back again. I told them the master's not here, he's in Port Harcourt. They said, yes, they know, but he's coming back today. After four or five of them said the same thing, I figured they must be right and, obviously, they were. Here you are."

"But," my father asked, "how the heck could they possibly know if I didn't know it myself until a few hours ago?"

"Didn't you ever hear of the bush telegraph? The drums, you know."

My mother asked him how the trip had gone and said she had missed him and had been worried when he didn't return on the day he said he would. She expressed concern that he hadn't been able to purchase the galena and wondered if they would be able to do business in Africa. She said life was dull in Lagos, despite the many unattached men who cast sheep's eyes at her. She had one gem to tell him, however.

"Do you remember those two English fellows who sat at the table next to ours in the dining room and who were always glad to accept your Chesterfields and a cup of our Nescafé, but never gave anything in return? You know, of course, that they were bursting with curiosity to know why we're here and what we're doing in British territory, but they had enough sense not to ask you. Well, the day you left, one of them asked me why you went to Port Harcourt."

"That wasn't very complimentary to you," my father said. "They must have thought you'd be foolish enough to give them information they knew they could never get from me. What did you tell them?"

My father was delighted with her reply. "I told them that Mr. Franklin went to Port Harcourt to get girls for the American slave market. I haven't seen them since. They must have been a couple of spies put next to us by one of the big European companies to get information about our business."

"Josie," he said with a laugh and a hug, "the tropics haven't dulled you a bit."

Chapter 11

▼▼▼▼▼▼

My Parents

My mother's childhood was cloaked in mystery for me. She was born in Manhattan in 1907 but grew up in Akron, Ohio. Her father, Arthur, an immigrant from Russia via Canada, made and lost several fortunes. I have a photo of my mother, her sister, Henrietta, who was two years older, and their two older brothers, sitting in their car that my mother said was the first one in Akron. When my mother was little, she was sent to live with her grandmother for a few months when her mother was too sick to care for her. This was a really unhappy time for her, especially because, for some reason, they told her that her mother was her sister.

My mother was artistic, and in the sixth grade the teacher told her that if she didn't stop doodling, she would have to repeat the grade. She didn't stop and she repeated sixth grade. My grandmother died when my mother was a sophomore in college. That was when she fled her unhappy home and transferred from the University of Ohio to

Cornell University. Being a shy young woman, she didn't affiliate with her sorority, Alpha Epsilon Phi, on the new campus. She didn't want to subject herself to the possibility of rejection, nor did she want them to have to take her.

My mother was a very talented artist and was the first liberal arts student that Cornell permitted to take a fine arts class, figure drawing. Her drawings were very sensitive and beautiful and looked like an old master had done them. She graduated from Cornell in 1929 and roomed with her sister, Henrietta, in New York City, where they were lucky to get work as secretaries. My mother always said that a degree in English was not the most useful thing to get, since the world was not waiting for yet another English major.

In addition to her art talent, she was an excellent seamstress and she designed and made a lot of her own clothes. She could also whistle beautifully and mirror-write. With a pencil in each hand she could simultaneously write her name in script, forward with the right hand and, starting with the letter "J" for Josephine, backwards with her left hand.

She was very pretty and petite with long dark hair, a slender nose that curved slightly upward, smooth skin, and sensuous lips, and younger men were always asking her out because she didn't look her age. Several years after she had graduated from Cornell, a date took her to a Brown-Cornell football game and there she met my father. Smitten by her beauty, he managed to get her telephone number and he called her the next day.

My father was slim and handsome with short, dark,

He called her the next day

curly hair and an intense brooding look. Two weeks after they met he bought a wedding ring, although they didn't get married for another two years because of the Depression. They were married by a judge on New Year's Day, 1936, in her brother's apartment in Manhattan.

My father, who was two years younger than my mother, had just received his law degree from Yale. Six years after their marriage he got a job working for the State Department in Washington, D.C. in the Alien Property Custodian office. The goal of the agency was to prevent the Axis powers–Germany, Japan and Italy–from using the assets of governments and nationals of occupied countries for their war purposes. My mother was working in another wing of the same building and they could wave to each other from the windows in their offices. My father's boss at the State Department thought marriage was a refuge for the weak, so they felt they had to keep their marriage a secret. After a few years of living with my father, my mother told Hen that, far from being a refuge for the weak, you needed to be strong to be married. I recall her saying to him on a number of occasions over the years, "I won't be your doormat."

My father was particularly proud of the Phi Beta Kappa key he had earned at Brown and wore it every day on his key chain. He even had replicas made as earrings for my mother and a charm for her bracelet. He could recite each grade he'd gotten at Brown, course by course and semester by semester. An exasperated high school teacher had once told him he would never graduate from high school, so that made the Phi Beta Kappa key all the sweeter.

When my father graduated from law school in 1934, in the middle of the Depression, there weren't a lot of jobs to be had for Jews, as they usually were only hired by Jewish law firms, so he became somewhat embittered about being Jewish. Though he had been bar mitzvahed, he eventually turned his back on his religion, Americanizing his first name, changing it from Leo to Lee. After marrying my mother, he changed his last name, Friedman, as well, taking hers—Franklin—which had also been changed.

When I was grown and asked my mother what her original family name was, she insisted that Franklin was the only one she had ever known. But she admitted that her father had changed his first name from Adolph to Arthur, during the Second World War, for obvious reason. Together, my parents became Quakers after being introduced to the religion by their sister-in-law, Virginia.

Although they had very little money, they managed to rent a lovely house in Alexandria, Virginia, where they were living when I was born in Washington, D.C. My father used to say that since I was born below the Mason-Dixon Line I cried with a Southern accent, so he called me Dixiebelle and my mother Honeychild.

They lucked into buying a dark green Rolls Royce at a low price from a friend who was desperate to unload it. They said they didn't have a pot to cook in but they drove around looking like the millionaires that they weren't, enjoying the status that came with the image. They were friends with a sophisticated bunch of people, including a man who was engaged to Ginger Rogers until his family broke it up. The parents felt that an actress was not the right sort of person for their son.

As an extra source of income from his State Department job, my father handled a legal case for another friend named Richard Pousette-Dart. Richard had no money at the time, so in lieu of payment, he made a series of photographs of my mother and painted a portrait in black and white of her "soul." He pursued his art career and went on to become very successful, with several of his paintings hanging in the Metropolitan Museum and a posthumous

The Rolls

one-man show at the Guggenheim Museum in 2007. The portrait of my mother always had a place of honor over the mantel wherever we lived.

My mother used to say that my father should have been a teacher, since he really enjoyed explaining things. He had stories from his childhood that he would tell me at bedtime as he rubbed my back, like the time he and Sidney fell through the ice up to their knees when they were eight and ten. I would beg my father to tell that story over and over because he made it sound funny, with wonderful approximations of what the ice sounded like as their legs broke through it. He enjoyed singing and taught me favorite songs from his camp counselor days and from his law school alma mater. "The Whiffenpoof Song" was probably his most beloved song.

My father loved to read and introduced me to the Penrod books by Booth Tarkington. He would describe a book by Mark Twain, laughing at the stories and encouraging me to read them. I didn't always read the books he recommended, but that didn't discourage him because he enjoyed the act of teaching and describing. When I floundered with my schoolwork he would pump me up with suggestions and help, perhaps too much help at times, because some of my writing sounded suspiciously like my father had written it, which he had.

After they married, my mother became a little overweight, due, she said, to serving duck for dinner too often, and my father became fond of saying, "When our weights meet, we part." When she would see an overweight woman my mother would anxiously ask my father, "Am I as fat as she is?"

"I don't think so, I'm not sure," he would reply, not very reassuringly.

She was terribly conscious of her weight and appearance and she would say to me, "Regard me as the horrible example." She often warned me not to eat for the wrong reasons, like comfort or reward, and told me I didn't have to clean my plate. The really strange thing is that when I look at the photos of my mother, she doesn't look overweight—not fat, not thin, just right—and yet, sadly, we always thought of her as fat.

My parents didn't want to be called "Mommy" and "Daddy," although that's what I called them. If I was talking about one of them to the other, I referred to them as Lee and Josie. When some hapless person got out their baby photos to show my father, it was a source of pride and amusement to him that he would show them a cat's whisker that he carried in his wallet. It was his anti-proud-par-

Better a dirty baby alive than a clean baby dead

ent statement to show he was above it all.

My mother said that the only time in her life she wasn't lonely was when she was pregnant. Unfortunately for my mother, after holding off starting a family for eight years, she got a sickly baby. I spent most of my first year in the hospital recovering from asthma, croup, allergies to turpentine when the painters were working on our house, and a doll in my crib that was filled with sawdust. The doctor told her not to give me a full bath my first year. "Better a dirty baby alive than a clean baby dead," he warned.

Chapter 12

▼▼ ▼▼ ▼▼ ▼▼ ▼▼

Reunited

Summer vacation was half over. And so, about four months after I had arrived at Farnaby, Mrs. French told Albert and me that we would be joining our parents in Africa at the end of July. The girls from the school would be returning for the fall semester soon, and finally, our parents had requested our presence. We would be flying together to Nigeria and Albert would continue on to the Gold Coast, now called Ghana.

As we packed up our belongings Albert cried. He said he was sad to be leaving, but I certainly wasn't and thought he might be faking it to be polite. On the other hand, maybe he had trepidations, because he had only seen his parents twice in the past three years. I considered feigning sadness, but since I was really elated to be with my parents again, I wasn't going to pretend otherwise. A few days later we said good-bye to Omar and Beatrice and left for the airport.

Boarding the BOAC plane in the afternoon, the two of us traveled unescorted, the six-year-old and the eight-year-old, and flew through the night. If Albert really had been sad, he certainly didn't appear to be once on the plane. Later in the evening we annoyed some of the other passengers who were trying to sleep, giggling in the darkened plane, making up our own words to "Good King Wenceslas" and singing quietly:

Albert bumped into a wheelbarrow,
Said I beg your pardon.

The stewardess came over and, putting a finger on her lips, motioned us to stop.

I arrived in Nigeria late the next morning, still wearing my gray wool uniform. Gathering my belongings, I said good-bye to a sleepy Albert and walked down the steps of the plane and into a wall of damp heat. The musty, earthy smell of the tropics assaulted me, an odor that always reminds me of Africa.

A barefoot airport official led everyone who had disembarked to customs in a shed that was separated from the rest of the airport by a chicken-wire fence. We were required to stay there while we were being processed, but I looked through the wire and saw my parents standing just outside the enclosure. This was the moment I had dreamed about and then given up all hope for, and there were my parents, so near and yet so far. I tried to run to them, but the airport staff wouldn't let me. They smiled and waved to me, and I tried hard to be brave and not cry, but the tears came against my will, and after a few minutes the customs official took pity and let me through to them.

"Dixiebelle, we missed you," my father said as he hugged me.

I could see my mother struggling with her emotions, but instead of trying to talk, she just held me close. It was overwhelming to finally be together again. They looked just as I had tried to picture them so many times at Farnaby.

After my tears had dried, we got my suitcase and drove in the Buick to the house my parents had rented, while I told them all about Farnaby. Half an hour later we pulled up in front of a white Mediterranean-style villa that was owned by a British couple on leave in England. The house came with six servants, or six headaches, as my mother called them.

We sat down for lunch in the dining room and my mother pressed the buzzer on the floor with her foot to signal to the maid that we were ready to eat. Out came a bounty of food.

England was in such a bad way because of the war and still had rationing of basic items like milk, butter, meat, sugar, eggs, and chocolate. Now here I was in the land of plenty.

"Isn't it rationed?" I asked in my newly acquired English accent when I saw butter, meat, and fresh vegetables. My mother sucked in her breath and I think that moment was when she realized the enormity of what they had done, leaving me in a boarding school in post-war England for more than four months. I hadn't had a decent meal since I had been dropped off at Farnaby.

After lunch my mother showed me around the house.

The house in Lagos

This was a far cry from our two-bedroom apartment in Jackson Heights with no servants. It was beautiful, with a carport at the front door, and a roomy center hall. The living room had French doors across the front wall. A large fireplace had lit electric logs to simulate fire for homesick Englishmen. Several small translucent lizards that lived on the wall above the fireplace were allowed to stay because they ate insects. They were about six inches long from head to tail and when you got close to them you could almost see the wall through their panting little bodies. Since there were no screens on the windows or doors the lizards performed an important function.

At the far end of the living room was a covered, open porch. Off the living room was a small, cozy library with books and a record player. To the right of the center hall was the dining room with a table, ten chairs, and a sideboard. There was a wood-burning stove and oven in the kitchen, but no refrigerator. In order to keep food, especially sugar, away from the voracious ants it needed to be packed up tightly or stored in a tin. It was a constant battle of man versus insects.

The back of the dining room looked onto a scrubby yard with a small building for the servants' quarters. There were alligator pear trees (avocado), paw paw trees (papaya), and mango trees. All of these fruits were new to me; I would come to hate the mangoes because they were stringy, but the avocados and papayas were delicious. Best of all, there were seven chickens, which I would name after the Seven Dwarfs and chase around the property.

Upstairs were two bedrooms, each with its own bathroom. My parents' room was large and had an open covered porch at the far end. One day, during a very heavy rain, my mother and I were sitting on their bed and she was teaching me to play gin rummy as we listened to the rain crash down on the tin roof. It was so noisy we could barely hear ourselves say, "Gin."

My room was smaller and had only two pieces of furniture: an armoire with an interior light that stayed on all the time to prevent mold from forming on clothes and shoes, and a four-poster bed in the middle of the room with mosquito netting. At bedtime my father or mother would perch inside the netting with me and rub my back as we talked.

"You're nothing but skin and bones," my father would say fondly. "And you have long legs and pretty hair. You're going to break a lot of hearts when you get older."

I laughed at his compliments, believing I was, indeed, a beautiful little girl. Before he left the room he would sing "Goodnight, Irene."

Then he settled the mosquito netting around the bed, but after he was gone and I was lying there, I heard the whining of the mosquitoes searching for their victim, sometimes outside the net and sometimes inside with me.

If my mother was in her room, I could hear her singing "The Man I Love" as she dressed for a dinner party they were hosting, or an evening out.

Some day he'll come along
The man I love
And he'll be big and strong
The man I love ...

Maybe I was reading into it, but I heard a sadness in her voice as she sang it. Perhaps that was the way it was meant to sound, but it's the only song I can ever remember her singing, the only song I associate with my mother.

Between my room and my parents' room there was a mysterious locked closet that my mother said contained things of the owners that they wanted to keep private and separate. There was something a little scary and intimidating about a locked closet and I stared curiously at it when I passed by.

One morning, after I had been there two weeks, I awoke to frantic screaming and banging. I leapt from my bed and ran downstairs in my pajamas. All six servants were on the porch outside the living room with brooms, banging and swiping at hundreds of huge, fat, ugly flying roaches that were at least two inches long. The windows and doors had been closed to prevent the bugs from getting into the house. My mother said that in preparation for building a house next door, the contractor had set the field on fire and all the roaches had left there and escaped to our house. It was so horrifying that I turned to my mother and said the unthinkable: "Maybe I'll go back to England." In later years, whenever my mother told the story of what I had said, she always sounded amused.

The invasion went on for hours but eventually the onslaught slowed and then stopped and the servants swept up the dead roaches and life returned to normal. Never again did I mention returning to England.

At one of my parents' dinner parties, everyone was gathered in the living room enjoying cocktails. The lights behind the logs were turning and glowing red, and the lizards on the wall around the fireplace were still, except for an occasional twitch of their body and a snap of their tongue if an insect came close.

As the guests sipped their Pimm's Cups from glass-bottomed pewter mugs and their gin and tonics, the talk turned to servants. First checking that the maid who was serving drinks was out of earshot, one of the guests, "Dicky" Bird, told about a reference he had given to a man he had fired. He had written, "This man is looking for a good berth. Give him a wide one." That way the servant wouldn't know he had been given a bad reference and there would be no reprisals.

After some laughter, my mother told about the servant who'd put my mother's bracelet into the garbage pail. If it wasn't noticed and nothing was said, after several days, out it would go with the garbage, to be retrieved by the servant.

My parents were now the employers of a chauffeur, two gardeners, a cook, and two servants who cleaned the house and served meals. Talk turned to how much people were paying their servants. "Don't overpay," my parents were cautioned by the woman my mother referred to as "Bird's Nest" because of her unruly upswept hair. "You'll spoil the market for everyone!"

My father said that when he asked a servant to pick up a paper outside the house, the man replied, "No, sah, that's not my job. I work inside." The downstairs man, called the downboy, only did chores downstairs; the upstairs maid only worked upstairs.

A story was told of an Englishman who had gone " 'round the bend." This was the big fear of all the whites who lived in Africa for a period of time. Either they might get some dread disease or they might lose their mind and go " 'round the bend." It's what made adhering to a routine of dressing for dinner and taking your anti-malaria medicine every day so important. If you got behind in your medicine you might get blackwater fever and go crazy or even die.

Some people were incredibly kind, and one of the men who worked at the American Embassy offered to lend me his little black Scottie. Donnie was very gentle and affectionate and my constant playmate as well as the bane of any African who rode by our house on a bicycle. When Donnie saw them coming along the road, he would race toward them, barking furiously, and they would pedal as fast as they could to get up speed and then put their bare feet on the handlebars until they were safely past.

Donnie loved to chase lizards, and one day while I was standing in the front hall, a large orange lizard came running in, with Donnie close behind. As I watched open-mouthed, they breezed past me, shot through the foyer, on into the living room and out an open French door.

All the whites belonged to the Ikoyi Club. The English, as well as Americans who worked for the embassy, and any expatriates and foreign nationals doing business there were members. That's where we met Joan Newman, her husband, and their daughter Deanne, who was my age. She was pretty, with short curly blond hair and big brown eyes. We played together in the pool at the club, and at her house. One day we were in her garden, having fun, laughing and making happy noise, when we decided to go upstairs to her bedroom. When we got to the top of the stairs, from out of nowhere, her mother's hand unexpectedly reached out and grabbed Deanne.

"Wait in Deanne's room, Alida," she said with cold fury in her voice and dragged my friend off. As I waited in Deanne's bedroom, I heard loud cries of fear and pain. What on earth could be happening? I didn't know what to do. I wanted to go and see what was wrong, but I was afraid to move, so I sat there with my hands over my ears, trying to drown out Deanne's screams.

It was horrible and continued for what seemed like forever. When Deanne rejoined me her eyes were red. There were welts on her arms and a slap mark on her cheek. Her hair and clothes were in disarray. Between sobs she told me her mother had been taking a nap and our laughter disturbed her, and she became so enraged that she beat up her daughter.

Deanne, aside from being an adorable, well-mannered kid, was with her parents only at Christmas and summer vacations. The rest of the year she was at school in England. It seemed especially cruel to treat her that way, when all we had been doing was playing. My parents had never spanked me—the only punishment I ever got was an occasional pinch from my mother. Sometimes, if she was really annoyed with me she would call me "Princess," her voice dripping with sarcasm. But beatings like the one Deanne received that day were unimaginable, as was her mother doing it when there was a guest to witness it.

Chapter 13

▼▼ ▼▼ ▼▼ ▼▼

Letter to Hen

Aug. 3, 1951

Dear Hen,

Alida is here with us now in that nice house I told you about that we're renting from the couple who went on leave. She flew down on the last day of July, and we're so glad to have her here—we had been counting the minutes. I think she had a hard time in England. She cried at the airport when she saw us, and we choked up, too. At her first meal here she asked if the food was rationed. She seems to be happy now, but doesn't know yet that we're planning to send her to another boarding school about 800 miles away. I hope she doesn't get too upset. We're holding off on telling her.

Because I was thirty-six when Alida was born (old to be having your first child), I've always been anxious for her to grow up and be self-sufficient.

When she's eighteen, I cut the apron strings, but for now, it's good to have us all together again.

This is a wild and woolly place, all right. It used to be called the Slave Coast, for obvious reasons. There are witch doctors and cannibals (no kidding), dense jungles and mangrove swamps. The jungle is impenetrable except by canoe on the numerous creeks that run down into the gulf. The creeks are used by tribes that fish for their livelihood and occasionally massacre each other in bitter inter-tribal wars over fishing rights.

The galena mining seems to be promising, although Lee is having problems getting his partners to keep him in funds to make purchases. It's a big headache for him.

And of course, there are insects and horrible, exotic diseases you can get from them, and wild animals. Kenya is the big-game country, but we also have our share of lions, baboons, bush dogs, hyenas, buffalo, antelope, and leopards. Of course, you never see these animals in Lagos because it's a city. But they're out there in the countryside.

Well, dear, that's all for now. Write back soon.
All my love,
Josie

Chapter 14

Lee and Sidney

Sidney wrote to my father that he was glad that I was now nearer to them than when I was in England, but hoped that within a short time my father would be able to set up his business so that he could run it from America.

"If you had a smart reliable man you could have him go there and do the job you're doing," Sidney wrote.

My father disagreed. He persisted in talking about how much "dough" he could make and said that he'd willingly stay on for a long time and maybe eventually have someone come over from America to assist him or take his place, but, until then, he'd keep plugging at it himself.

"If I can get a big batch of ore and my partners don't make the money available in time to purchase it," he told Sidney, "I'll let you in on the business and I'll even let Mom get into it." He said this as if it were some sort of investment that, of course, anyone would want to get involved in.

He was still hoping to dump his partners because, when he had asked them for more money once he began to make a profit, they had answered that he didn't need more money and that if he had it, he would only spend it.

He wrote to Sidney, "My partners probably will come through with the money, but their timing is bad and it's rough on my nervous system. When I'm able to get the goods I can't get the funding, and when I've got the funds, I can't get the goods."

A week later, cash was running dangerously low and my father panicked that his partners wouldn't come through with the money in time to make purchases. He cabled Sidney: "NEED ABOUT FIVE THOUSAND FOR SHORT PERIOD TO PURCHASE AVAILABLE ORE PLEASE REMIT BY CABLE WHATEVER YOU CAN."

Sidney sent $1000 from their mother and $1000 from himself. A few days later my father sent another cable: "THANKS FOR REMITTANCE PLEASE CABLE THREE THOUSAND MORE HAVE OVER TWEN-TY-FIVE TONS MONEY PERFECTLY SAFE".

"Your request for $3000 more is an unanswerable request," Sidney fumed in his next letter. "We just don't have that kind of money lying around and it is unfair for you to get us involved in transactions we can't possibly understand. Each letter implores us to send money and it makes us feel guilty if we don't send it to you.

"Furthermore, although you write in great detail what you're doing, I can't tell whether you're making money or losing money. Every letter we get from you is optimistic, but when the chips are down you finally end up with nothing, and each letter says you're on the verge of doing something, but you never seem to achieve it.

"Your profit has been too small for all the risks and hard work. I think it should be several hundred percent. Twenty per cent is nothing. If you can't make at least 100 per cent, my feeling is you ought to return here. Your life will certainly be a lot more normal and you'll be in a much better position to determine just where you're going at the age of forty-three."

My father's partners did eventually send funds, nothing like the $50,000 per month they had contracted to provide, but now that my father was temporarily over the sweat about money, his spirits rose.

His spirits were further buoyed when he received permission from the government to prospect for more ore, and he sent out a crew to find a viable mine to lease. He intended to expand into mining tin and columbite, an essential ingredient in the manufacture of jet planes.

He and my mother celebrated the government's permission to prospect by ordering champagne at the club. As the waiter popped the cork and they clinked glasses he said to my mother, "We're on our way! There's big dough in this business and I've made a start. Just because my partners have let me down, there's no reason for me to give up, and I'm going to hang on as long as I can." My mother, habitually more cautious, just sipped her champagne.

"I don't want to come home broke, with my tail between my legs, without capital to start a business," my father wrote to Sidney. "I'd rather cut my throat, figuratively speaking, than start looking for a job now that I've gotten used to being my own boss. I'm on my way up and I won't give up. I hope that no one in my family ever needs any financial assistance, but if they do, they can always count on me."

My father sent Animashaun to purchase galena from a distant chief who had said he could provide fifty tons of galena. After Animashaun had been in the bush for three weeks he cabled that he had bought fifteen tons and arranged for thirty-five more. He said that my father could expect two to three tons per day to arrive at the dock in Lagos. Finally, after two months of anxious waiting, nail-biting, and sleepless nights for my parents, Animashaun cabled that he could only rail down seven tons altogether. This was extremely disheartening news because output projections had been so optimistic.

Chapter 15

▼▼ ▼▼ ▼▼ ▼▼ ▼▼

Letter to Hen

Dec. 26, 1951

Dearest Hen,

Life goes on here in pretty much the same way since the last time I wrote—I'm doing better after my last bout with malaria, but I'm still not well and my blood count is down. I'm not trying to shield you, as you seemed to think I was from the comment in your last letter. I just don't see any purpose in going on about it.

Except for an occasional trip into the bush with Lee, I'm alone and lonely all day, bored and sometimes quite depressed. How did I ever get into this predicament? At least if we were making money, it might be worth it, but things just don't seem to work out and I wonder if they ever will. Lee had this idea that because he was white and American and smart, that he could pull it off, but Africa is winning. The best I can say for this past nine months is that it's interesting. That's what we've decided to tell people when we come back—it was interesting.

Thanks for sending the two girdles from Saks. I'll send you a check for $32.35 right away for them and the medicine you mailed. I can't send you enlargements of the beach pictures that you liked—there's no place here to make enlargements. Thank you for the Christmas gifts. But don't you think it was a little mean to send Alida the doll clothes that Jeannie had made for her own doll just because you got mad at her? Was she very upset about it?

I'm sorry the masks we sent were infested with African powder post beetles. I hope they don't end up infesting your whole apartment! If we send anything else, I'll treat them here first so that doesn't happen again.

As your loving sister, I wish I were there to help you deal with Burt regarding Father's will. Try to keep calm when you're talking to him, even if he upsets you. I agree, Father should have divvied up the money amongst the four us instead of lumping it all together and forcing us to deal with Burt ad infinitum. Try to save something of Father's from the apartment for me. I won't say anything to Burt—I'll let you handle it as you see fit. I keep wishing I had been there when Father died, both for you and for him.

About a week after Father died Alida said she would write to him. She had forgotten that he died, but remembered that I had asked her several times to write. I know that she really didn't want to—she told me she didn't know what to say and I guess that's my fault because she had barely ever seen him. The last time was in the nursing home before we left and he couldn't talk by then. Anyway, there was a long silence on my part and I know she felt terrible when she remembered he was gone.

I can't tell you how much it means to me that you would be willing to sell your stock and go back to work in order to help us out. I know how tight things are with you, and you know that I would never ask you for money if things weren't pretty bad. Even with Sidney's help, we're still just barely hanging on. I get panicky sometimes, being so far away and in such dire straits. We only have enough money for plane tickets to get from Africa to Europe, but not from Europe to America.

Well, I've complained enough for one letter. I'll try to be more positive the next time I write.

Much love, honey, many kisses and keep well.

Josie

Chapter 16

❧❧❧❧❧

Hillcrest School

"When a matured man discovers that he has been deserted by Providence, deprived of his God, and cast without help, comfort, or sympathy, upon a world which is new and strange to him, his despair, which may find expression in evil living, the writing of his experiences, or the more satisfactory diversion of suicide, is generally supposed to be impressive. A child, under exactly similar circumstances as far its knowledge goes, cannot very well curse God and die. It howls til its nose is red, its eyes are sore, and its head aches. Punch and Judy, through no fault of their own, had lost all their world. They sat in the hall and cried."

Baa Baa, Black Sheep, Rudyard Kipling

We found a boarding school here in Nigeria that you can go to and be much closer to us than you were in England," my father announced cheerily one morning at the breakfast table. "It's called Hillcrest, and it's for the children of American missionaries, so you won't be the only American."

"You're going to like it," he added. "The school's in Jos and the weather is more like Connecticut than Africa—it's cooler and dryer than Lagos. And you won't have to wear a uniform."

"But, Daddy, why can't I stay here with you?" I said, the tears immediately beginning to well.

"We wish you could, of course," he replied, "But there's no school for you here in Lagos."

"Do I have to leave soon?" I cried. "I'm not ready to go yet. I just got here. And I'll miss Donnie." I really loved that little dog and I had been together again with my parents for only about five weeks.

"No, you don't have to leave right away," my mother said. "Not 'til next week. We'll fly up to Jos and I'll take you to the school. I really think you're going like it," she said, unconvincingly.

A week later my clothes were packed, the reunion with my parents was over, and my father was driving my mother and me to the airport in Lagos. As we waited on the tarmac in the hot sun for the plane to arrive, a vendor came around selling jewelry. There were two Englishmen waiting with us, and when they saw my mother admiring a very heavy metal bracelet, one said to the other, "Pb."

"Lead," my mother said to me, loud enough for them to hear her. She didn't like the man to presume that she was ignorant of the symbol for lead and she wanted them to know she knew.

On the way to the next boarding school

While we waited for the plane my father took pictures of me in a dress with a tiny print that my mother had sewn, wearing sandals and socks and a headband. I was smiling shyly, lamb to the slaughter.

When the plane finally arrived, the two Englishmen, my mother, and I boarded. It was a tiny four-passenger plane that took almost four hours to fly the eight hundred miles to Jos. When we got there, my mother hired the only airport taxi to drive us to Hillcrest, which was about forty-five minutes away.

We were greeted by Mrs. Wine, the wife of the headmaster. She showed us around a large building that housed the quarters for the younger boys and girls, the dining room, and the Sunday parlor. There were several smaller buildings where the older girls and boys roomed. Down a long dirt driveway were two classrooms for the lower grades. Classrooms for the older kids were elsewhere on the grounds.

I saw children playing games. Just as when I had entered Farnaby, the school year was already well under way. It seemed I was always coming into the middle of things. After Mrs. Wine had shown us around, my mother hugged and kissed me good-by. As I started to cry, she left in the waiting taxi that had brought us. Mrs. Wine asked if I would like to join in the games with the other children.

"Can I lie down?" I asked timidly.

"If you like," she answered and led me to a dorm room.

Devastated at being left off again, I just wanted to be alone, and was surprised but grateful when she let me. I lay in the dark room with five or six beds, crying for my parents and wishing I were back in Lagos, until I finally fell asleep. The next morning I dragged myself out of bed with everyone else and got dressed for breakfast. While the other girls seemed friendly, I was lost in a fog of homesickness.

My fourth grade class was in a room that had grades three through six, one row of seats with about six kids for each grade. Since most of the other children were American, no one made fun of my American accent, which had returned after a few weeks with my parents. Most of the parents and the Wines were Christian missionaries, so it was a very religious environment. I couldn't even say, "Darn!" without Esther, a girl my age, gasping and saying, "Where's the needle?" or "Darn the sock?"

We had prayer every morning in the classroom, and were supposed to close our eyes, but sometimes one of the kids would report that another hadn't closed his eyes.

"How do you know," the teacher would ask the tattler, "if your eyes were closed?"

On Sunday evenings about twenty-five of us would gather in the parlor for prayer and hymns. Afterwards the Wines would say, "Who wants to go first?"

Hands would shoot up and someone would tell how he or she had "become a Christian," always involving an epiphany about God and Jesus. Later, when I told her about this, my mother said that they were born Christians and didn't "become." I guess she missed the subtleties of "born again" Christians. Toward the end of the meetings they showed films regarding the sins of alcohol, one of which had a woman crying because she had knowingly eaten ice cream that was made with whiskey. Another movie showed a girl very upset because she had chewed bubble gum made with beer.

Much later, when I was with my parents again, I told my mother about the two films.

"Ice cream won't freeze if it's made with alcohol, and no company makes bubblegum with beer," she pointed out. She was always ready to debunk the myths of the missionaries and keep me from being taken in by their propaganda.

I was scared of a boy named Rufus. He was my age and when he was younger he had touched a live wire and burned off parts of his fingers. His hands were a horrifying sight and if you did something he didn't like or if you said something mean about his fingers he would run after you, trying to touch you with his stumps, yelling, "I'll suffer you." I only made that mistake once. After that I was unfailingly polite to Rufus.

I learned how harsh Mr. Wine could be one Saturday when I started to straighten the orange crate that was my little cubby in the dorm. I took my clothing out and laid it on the bed, and was half-way through folding and putting it back, when I went down the hall to visit my best friends, Hazel and Melody. I wasn't there long when Mr. Wine appeared in the doorway of their room, interrupting our laughter, his face red with anger. He pointed at me.

"You left your room in a mess," he roared. "Get back there right away and straighten up."

With Mr. Wine on my tail, yelling, "Faster!" and smacking my bottom every few steps, I raced back to the scene of my terrible crime and set things to rights. They had caning at Hillcrest School, too, but this was the closest I ever came to being punished. Once again, as at Farnaby, I lived in fear of doing anything that might bring the wrath of the school administration down on my head and backside.

Classroom hours were from eight-thirty to four o'clock, with a one-hour rest period after lunch. Sometimes during rest hour, the teacher would have me grade papers while she rested on my bedroll. An Australian girl and I were made to carry buckets of water from a sink in the classroom closet out to the girls' room to fill the toilet tanks. When I was with my parents again I finally got to tell them what was going on. They asked the Australian girl about it and she corroborated my story, adding that the buckets, when filled with water were "koinda heavy-loike." My parents complained to the school and that put an end to our days as toilet-tank fillers.

Every afternoon around four o'clock we were served cookies and milk, outside in nice weather, in the main building on a rainy day. They lined up rows of glasses of milk and delicious-looking cookies but, in order to get the cookie, you had to drink the milk and the milk was boiled. Boiling was the only way to eliminate bacteria but, when boiled, it formed a skin on top and I couldn't stand the skin. I longed for the cookie, but for a year and a half I hid at snack time and didn't drink any milk.

One night at dinner an older boy at my table asked me what my father did for a living. I was prepared for this question, as my parents had told me never to tell what he did, and what to say when asked. I felt a little funny, but I repeated what they had instructed me to say:

"What would be of interest I could not tell you. What I could tell you would not be of any interest."

He gave me a puzzled look and tried again, but I repeated my answer and refused to say any more than that. I never understood what the big secret was, but I grew up believing that people had sinister motives if they asked what kind of work you did.

Even though I was eight, for reasons unknown, the Wines decided to move me out of my dorm and down to the end of the hall with the five-year-olds. I don't know why they put me there, but I liked the little girls and enjoyed having an audience and making them laugh. One day, at rest hour, I was clowning around and Alice, the girl in the bunk above mine, was laughing at my antics, and she laughed so hard that she tumbled off her bed. She hit the cement floor head first and lay there without moving. Someone ran and got the Wines, and they took her away to the hospital. I never saw her again, nor did I learn if or how she was recovering. I was overwhelmed with guilt and remorse. I blamed myself completely for the accident. If I hadn't made her laugh so much she wouldn't have fallen. No one else ever said it was my fault, but they didn't have to.

After that, I became the keeper of order. If anyone so much as whispered during rest hour I would make all of them get off their beds and stand in a row. I said mean things to them and I was too young to understand why I was doing it. Eventually, along with feeling guilty for the harm that had come to Alice, I began to feel guilty for being mean to the little girls, who were all so nice. I eased up on them and on myself and began to feel a little better about my role in the accident but I never completely exorcised the feeling that I had done something terribly wrong.

Hazel and Melody asked me to be part of a little joke they wanted to play and, happy to be in on something fun, I agreed. Hazel said, "We're going to come to your dorm room and say in front of the girls that we heard that your room was being noisy. You say, 'That's a lie.' " I wasn't sure where the joke in this was, but I agreed to play along.

A few minutes later they came to my room and said in unison, "We heard that your room was being noisy," and, following along with the plan, I answered, "That's a lie." And they said "-da". In other words, "That's a-lie-da." My name.

Then they ran off laughing at their little joke—that turned out to be on me. I stood there for a few minutes while the joke sank in. Their little caper put a damper on our friendship for the rest of the time I was there.

In one of my mother's letters she wrote that she had sent me some cookies. I waited about a week and finally summoned up the nerve at dinnertime to approach the headmaster's table where the faculty ate.

"Mrs. Wine," I said, "my mother wrote that she had mailed some cookies to me. Have they arrived yet?"

"Oh, yes, dear," she replied, "they've arrived and I'm holding them for you."

"When can I have them?" I asked.

"I'll let you know," she said.

I stood there, hesitantly, not knowing what else I could say to get my mother's treat. Then I said, very politely, "Mrs. Wine, would you like to have some cookies?"

This produced laughter that rippled around the faculty table. About two weeks later the school newspaper came out and as I began reading it, my eye was caught by my name on one of the pages. It read:

Alida: Mrs. Wine, my mother wrote that she had mailed some cookies to me. Have they arrived yet?

Mrs. Wine: Yes, dear, they've arrived and I'm holding them for you.

Alida: When can I have them?

Mrs. Wine: I'll let you know.

Alida: Mrs. Wine, would you like to have some of my cookies?

I read and reread the words in disbelief. How could this have been printed in the school paper for all the world to see? Obviously, it was supposed to be some kind of humor at my expense, to show that I was trying to manipulate the Wines into letting me have my sweets. Eventually, I did get one or two cookies—I assumed the rest were eaten by the school staff and Mrs. Wine.

In my classroom I found a book of short stories by Rudyard Kipling with a title that caught my eye. "Baa Baa, Black Sheep" was a story about two children, Punch and his younger sister, Judy, who lived in India and were lovingly cared for by their parents and *ayah*. They were the apple of everyone's eye, but their parents had to send them to stay in England because the father's business had fallen on hard times and the parents couldn't keep the children with them. The caretaker in England loved little Judy, who was three, but hated five-year-old Punch. He was tormented and beaten by the caretaker and her son and called "Black Sheep."

Punch's heart was broken, not just because he missed his parents and the woman was so cruel, but because he was only allowed to have limited time with Judy. He became almost completely blind from reading too much, which was the only thing he was allowed to do. When their mother finally came to rescue them almost five years later, she was devastated by the harm that had come to her son and she begged his forgiveness.

I read that story over and over and each time I would break down. I was Punch, abandoned to a harsh and un-loving world. Would I ever live with my parents again? Would they beg *my* forgiveness for the pain they had caused?

My father wrote to Sidney, "The kid is happy at the new boarding school. All *I* need to be happy and well is suffi-cient tonnage of galena and enough money to pay for it."

Chapter 17

♦ ♦ ♦ ♦ ♦

Letter to Hen

Dec.15, 1951

Dear Hen,

If you noticed, we have a new address now. After six months, the owner of the house in Lagos that we were living in returned and the only place we could go was back to the Olympic Hotel, which is expensive and depressing. We decided to get a house in Jos, where Alida's school is, so Lee could be closer to the mines. We hadn't seen or spoken to her in half a year.

We're now at the Hill Station in Jos, 800 miles north of Lagos. It's a charming British inn with lovely gardens and very pleasant accommodations. The best thing is that it's near Alida's school, so she's living with us again and we drive her to school each day. It's run by American missionaries and is mostly for the children of missionaries.

I think they can be harsh, so thank God we have her with us.

Lee says things are going fairly well with the mining, and he's hopeful that soon he'll be able to turn a profit. We now have three galena mines, but he's finding it rough going to achieve the goal of 100 tons a month. He's having problems with the rains filling up the mine pits, and he could really use earth-moving equipment and trucks. But there's no money for that, and I wonder how he can continue to be so optimistic. Also, the partners are still withholding the money he needs to make purchases and to live, so Sidney has had to tide us over. We've been here almost a year and I wonder when we're actually going to show a profit.

We visited some friends in a place called Kaduna Falls. It was a long ride to get there, but worth it, as their house has a spectacular view of the falls and the most beautiful English gardens. They also had a gorgeous Blue Point Siamese cat. They're very rare and have a bluish, lavender tinge to their fur and blue eyes. Alida was enraptured, as was I.

Last week we visited another friend, Tommy Dodd, who has a large black horse named Marie that he brought into the living room, much to our shock! We were terrified that the horse might go to the bathroom right there but thank goodness she didn't! But poor Alida! He didn't serve dinner until ten o'clock (very continental of him) and she was ravenous. Being a bachelor, he didn't seem to notice and I was too embarrassed to ask if he had something she could nibble on. Then by ten o'clock she was so sleepy she could barely eat. The missionaries are such strange, suspicious people. If two people are engaged and want to return to the States for their wedding, they're not allowed to travel on the same ship for fear that they'll have sex. And they have an air about them that makes you feel they're looking down on everyone who's not one of them.

Write back soon.
All my love,
Josie

Bonding with a cat

Chapter 18

❧ ❧ ❧ ❧ ❧

The Hill Station

When I left Hillcrest as a boarding student, I went to live with my parents at the Hill Station. The main house had whitewashed walls and dark wood trim, about ten bedrooms, a pub with a large dark shiny wooden bar, a billiard room, a formal dining room with starched white tablecloths, and beautiful well-tended English rose gardens. The garden in the back of the hotel looked out on a magnificent vista of the surrounding countryside from the top of a hill. After a few weeks, we moved from the main house into one of the thatched roof cottages that had two bedrooms, a bathroom and a living room.

My father drove me to Hillcrest every morning and picked me up at four o'clock. Now that I was with my family and no longer in the tender clutches of the Wines, the weekends were mine and on Saturday my parents would drive me to one of the two bookstores in town, both missionary-owned. One was the Sudan Interior Mission

Lee and Alida at the Hill Station

Book Store and the other was the Church of the Brethren Mission Book Store. They had a good selection of novels, both religious and non-religious. The theme of the religious books, which I enjoyed, was generally about how someone who hadn't been such a good person found God and became a better and happier person.

My favorite book was the 1953 edition of *Picture Show Annual: For People Who Go to the Pictures*. On the cover was a photo of Anna Neagle and Michael Wilding in *Derby Day*. It was printed in England, but had full-page pictures of all the biggest stars—Frank Sinatra, Lana Turner, Cary Grant, Elizabeth Taylor. I would pore over the book, reading and re-reading it endlessly. I wanted to be a movie star, too.

There were two curiosities for me in town. One was the blind leper with diseased eyes and some missing fingers. There were several lepers, but this one, even with disfigurements, was magnificent in his long white robes and pure white horse, which he rode slowly about the town. The other curiosity was a family of albinos, with pinkish-white translucent skin and kinky yellow-white hair. The son was fat and I was fascinated, and also horrified, by him. I wondered what his life was like: Were the other African kids mean to him? Did he have friends, or was he an outcast?

Like many girls my age, I was in love with horses, and an African chief my father was doing business with gave me a horse. With all the free time I had on weekends, I had sobbed my way through *Black Beauty* over and over. How I wanted to name the horse Black Beauty, but he was dappled beige and so I had to settle for calling him Beauty. After school and on the weekends, my parents would drive me to the polo field, where we were boarding Beauty, and I would bring a lump of sugar or a carrot and he would eat it greedily. My happiest times were spent riding him around the polo field while the loudspeaker played "The Mexican Hat Dance." Usually I had the whole field to myself, although occasionally a polo player would show up for practice.

I started learning to jump with the groom coaching me. I was making good progress, but one day when Beauty and I cantered up to a low jump, at the last second he swerved to the right, and I lost my balance. Instead of making me fall, his sudden change of direction swung me around to the front of his neck, and, without a rider on his back and no one holding the reins, he began galloping. I clung tightly to his neck because if I had let go, he would have galloped right over me. That's how we arrived back at the stable, where he came to a sudden stop with me hanging off the front of him, my arms and legs in a death grip.

I unwound myself from Beauty's neck and stood up, shaken by my wild ride. With an effort I pulled myself together, took some deep breaths, jiggled my arms and legs and looked up to see my parents running toward me with a scared look.

Beauty and Alida

"Alida, are you all right?" My mother's worst fears about horseback riding had come true. "What on earth made him do that?" she exclaimed. Both my parents looked distraught and my father said, "I think that's enough for today, don't you?"

Everyone who has ever ridden knows that when you fall off, you have to get right back up. If you don't, you might never have the guts to ride again, so even though I really didn't want to, I said, "I have to take him out again." With the groom's help I climbed back up on Beauty.

"He's trembling," I said.

"Are you sure you're not the one who's trembling?" my mother asked, but after my parents and the groom examined him more closely they saw that Beauty really was shaking all over. I dismounted and the groom put him back in his stall. The next day my parents had the vet at the stable. He examined Beauty and shook his head. He took a vial of blood to analyze and then he called my father with the results.

He reported that Beauty had African tick fever and said that he'd probably had it for about a month, and that that was the reason he'd made a beeline back to the stable. He just didn't feel well enough to be ridden, let alone to jump. Then he added that tick fever was quite serious and usually fatal.

My father told me I wouldn't be riding Beauty while they treated him. The vet put Beauty on a regimen of antibiotics and they tried to fatten him up, but as I waited anxiously for good news over the next few weeks, his condition worsened. On one of the saddest days of my life my parents told me that they would have to put Beauty to sleep.

The African chief who had given him to me offered to take him back, but the vet told my mother that the chief would sell him to an Ibo tribe. He said they would use Beauty in a ceremony and beat him to death, then, just before he died, they would cut out his liver. How I wish my mother had never told me because the image of Beauty and all the other horses that had been tortured and would be tortured haunted my dreams for years, as did "The Mexican Hat Dance." Maybe she felt that was the only way I could accept his euthanization. I certainly didn't want him to suffer in a cruel African ceremony, but for years I blamed my parents for having him killed.

Before Beauty got sick, we visited friends who owned a pony named Brownie that they kept at their house. I rode Brownie that day, but he was a feisty little guy who unexpectedly bucked me off and then dragged me around the riding ring with my foot caught in the stirrup, and I ended up covered in bumps and scrapes.

I was devastated and feeling very low about Beauty when, a few weeks after he died, the friends offered to give me Brownie. Even though I knew I would never love him the way I had loved Beauty, I was glad to accept their offer. I renamed him Pixie and we boarded him at the polo field where we had boarded Beauty. He was a rich golden brown with a mane that stuck straight up, and though he was much smaller than Beauty, he had the devil in him. My mother used to sit in the car while I rode and watch nervously because you never knew when Pixie was go-

You never knew when Pixie was going to buck

ing to buck. I thought there was something comical about him, but at the same time, I didn't trust him and was always cautious when I was around him.

Around the time that I got Pixie, a brother and sister arrived at Hillcrest School who were not children of American missionaries. They were Irish, with freckles and blond hair, and thick brogues. When they learned that I had a pony, they started showing up at the polo field to ride Pixie and told the groom I had said they could. I didn't realize what they were doing until the groom told me they were coming to the stable on days I wasn't there.

That turned out to be the explanation for why the boy

would come up to me at school and say, "Air you coomin' to the field today?" It really upset me that they were riding my pony behind my back and it was very hard for me to ask them to stop, but, after much agonizing, I summoned the courage to tell them that they couldn't do it any more. I didn't want to hurt their feelings, but it wasn't as if they were my friends. I had had no contact with them other than for the boy asking if I was coming to the field that day.

Fortunately, I was an enthusiastic reader, because I didn't have any children to play with on the weekends or after school. I did have a friend my age who was also a day student at Hillcrest, and drove with us occasionally to and from school. She was a chubby, pretty Indian girl named Nirmbla Salawni. I could never get my father to stop pronouncing her name as it was spelled. I told him over and over that her name was pronounced "Nimla", but to no avail—"Nirmbla" it was for my father.

Nirmbla was also nine and almost since the day she was born she had been engaged to a boy back in India. I tried to imagine what it would be like to have someone pick out your husband and to marry a person you had never even met. What if you didn't like each other?

Nirmbla and I got along well for the most part and she didn't live far away from me, but, for some reason, we never played together after school. Outside of going to the club, there weren't a lot of things to do in Jos, so horse shows were really big. I signed up to compete in a gymkhana and Pixie and I practiced for weeks for the bending race and the potato race. The bending race consisted of riding your horse in and out of six poles like a slalom, and the first rider back at the starting line won. The potato race consisted of plucking a potato from the top of the six poles, one potato at a time, and then racing back to the beginning and dropping it in a bucket. The first one back with all their potatoes in the bucket was the winner. I was elated when I won the blue ribbon.

We had lived out in the countryside at the Hill Station for several months when management told us we had to leave. I figure one of three things had happened: either my parents could no longer afford it, something bad had occurred between my father and the proper British owners, or, as my parents told me, management policy was that the Hill Station was not for long-term stays. At any rate, my parents found a hotel in town, and we moved in.

Chapter 19

Letter to Hen

Apr. 1952

Dear Hen,

We've moved again, not for the better, and are now in the Pax Hotel. It's owned and run by a Syrian family. We've reached a low point, right on the edge of a shantytown. A white woman can't go walking around alone, not even to take a short walk.

With Lee gone all day and no place to go it's going to be hard to occupy myself until we pick Alida up at school. I wish I had learned to drive, but it really wouldn't be safe to go anywhere alone in case the car broke down. So I'm doing a lot of knitting and sewing and reading.

Sorry, I don't mean to complain, but you know how I like to keep busy with interesting projects, and I'm feeling trapped and isolated, even more than in the previous places we've stayed because this place is so awful. At least at the Hill Station I could walk around the grounds, and we had our own private bathroom. Here the toilets and tubs are down the hall and we have to share them with French whores and everyone else. And there's no one to talk to during the day. How I long to be home in America. I took my wonderful life there for granted, but if I ever get back there, I never will again.

On the bright side, it looks like things may work out, after all. We've gotten a chunk of money from the partners, and Lee says that our new leases will yield a good amount of galena. He's feeling very optimistic right now and consequently, so am I. Sidney keeps writing that we should come back to America, but since Lee doesn't want to come back broke, I'm afraid it's going to be a while before we return. Maybe this time things will work out. I hope so! Lee needs a new watch, but will hold off a bit before spending money on non-essentials.

It's been raining a lot and water dripped on Lee's desk in this wonderful hotel, so he had to quick move the typewriter and papers to a safe spot. We're out of film for the camera, and Jos is so primitive we can't get the film size that we need so I guess that means we won't be taking any pictures for a while.

Thanks for sending the rhinestones—they're for a cape I'm making for the costume ball. It's THE event of the season at the club, and I'm really looking forward to it and sewing feverishly to get my outfit done in time. It's fun being one of the few females around—it makes you feel quite special and you get a lot of attention, especially when you're almost the only American woman.

You're right—a man can just run out and pick up a woman, much easier than a woman can pick up a man. But you shouldn't say you're no longer attractive; it's just not true. How can you think of yourself as old—you're only two years older than I. An older woman can still be good-looking and sexy. Keep yourself up, put on makeup, do your hair and clothes, and just making the effort will make you feel better, I promise.

We're visiting friends this evening who have a small child, about one year old. The last time we saw her Lee made such a fuss over her, laughing and saying how cute she was. As for me I feel—it's a baby, no big deal. I really must tell him to tone it down in front of Alida so she doesn't feel slighted.

We're leaving in a few minutes to pick Alida up at school. We take her jodhpurs and boots with us and she changes in the car on the way to the polo field. I'll write again soon.

All my love,
Josie

Chapter 20

Letter to Sidney

May 20, 1952

Dear Sid:

Well, I am now beginning to approach the goal I originally planned on when I came here, and everything is going fine except, of course, for the fact that the price of lead has dropped a bit, but there is still a good margin of profit and besides, it might go up again.

In February I shipped fourteen tons; in March I shipped twenty-four tons; in April thirty-six tons, and before the month is over I expect to rail down to Lagos twenty to thirty tons; and the stuff is beginning to come in at the rate of over sixty to seventy tons a month, so I'm all right. However, I still have the same problem that most small business has—insufficient working capital. I'm down to about $400 total cash here, which is skating on pretty *thin ice. If Overseas Credit Corp. doesn't send me the advance they are supposed to send, then I'll be glad to accept your offer to let me have another couple of thousand. I should be in the clear and all set after two or three more shipments.*

Now the ore is beginning to roll in from the native mines. But the real gravy will be from my own. I expect word any day granting the lead mine to me, then I get the ore almost for nothing, though there will be plenty of hard work for me, which is what I came for.

We are well, though we took Alida out of school yesterday because a number of the kids have the mumps. The term ends May 30th, but they closed the school early on account of the mumps.

Nothing much to write about here. Fortunately, we can see American movies three times a week, if we want to go that often, and we go dancing a couple of times a month.

How do you feel and how is your family?

Regards to everyone,

Lee

Chapter 21

The Pax and the Club

The Pax Hotel was mean and low-down. We were their only long-term guests. I was the only child at the hotel for the eleven months we were there. The Pax was at the beginning of the native part of town and not nearly as nice as the Hill Station and we didn't have a cottage anymore—we only had two rooms. My mother and I shared a room, our two beds separated by a sink. My father's room was across the hall. With his indefatigable enthusiasm, my father found the one positive nugget to write home about our depressing hotel: he had been able to persuade the owners of the Pax to put screens on the windows of our two bedrooms so we no longer needed mosquito nets on the beds.

The walls inside and out were smooth white stucco with a dining room and bar on the first floor, and ten bedrooms on the second. On that same level there was a sitting room, two toilets, and two bathtubs, each in their own separate little room, for all the guests to share. When you wanted to take a bath, the hotel boys would march up and down the stairs, making multiple trips carrying buckets of hot water to fill the tub.

The Pax got a much more eclectic and colorful clientele than the proper English-owned Hill Station. It was populated with a never-ending stream of French prostitutes with see-through blouses and black bras, and seedy businessmen of all nationalities who drank before sundown. This was the dubious crowd with whom we shared the bathrooms and tubs.

The owners had a separate house behind the hotel with a novel burglar alarm system. Thousands of beer bottles piled upside down surrounded the foundation of their house, one on top of another, about three feet deep at the

A novel burglar alarm

Beer bottles delineate the garden beds

bottom and tapering off until they reached the windows, which were about four feet from the ground. If anyone wanted to break in they couldn't climb on the bottles: they would have had to remove them and if they removed more than a very few, all the bottles would come tumbling down and create a fierce racket. Still more beer bottles were placed upside down in the ground to delineate the beds of a very dry and unlovely garden. The kitchen was a tiny detached structure behind the hotel just large enough to hold a wood-burning stove and oven.

Dinner in the dining room at the Pax was most often mutton, a meat I came to loathe, served with fried onions, and flan for dessert. The topic of our dinner conversation was usually my father's experiences of the day. An exuberant storyteller, he would vividly describe what had happened, whom he had met, what everyone said, and it made for lively listening. With the vicious Mau Mau uprising unfolding in Kenya, sometimes my parents would discuss which of the hotel staff would be most likely to kill us and impale our heads on the fence post.

We adopted two of the hotel's cats, a calico we named Mother Cat and her son, a marmalade-colored long-haired beauty we called Ginger. They were my after-school companions at the hotel. Someone had long ago deposited a large mound of dirt at the back of the hotel and this became my playground. I built steps into the dirt and spent hours going up and down, pretending I was climbing a mountain or alternately, that it was a city I had built.

Across the street from the Pax was a school for African boys. Naked little boys and girls with distended bellies and huge belly buttons played in the street and peed in the open gutters. There were native-owned stalls that that we never went into, and down the block was a large store owned by Indians. It was like a bazaar; they carried almost everything you could want, from sunglasses and clothing to tools and house wares.

Jos is on a 4,000-foot-high plateau. That made it cool enough for us to wear a light coat on a fall evening, but warm enough in the daytime for the pagan women to walk naked along the roads with only a bunch of yellowing wilted leaves covering their crotches and intricately decorated calabashes on their heads, transporting items for sale.

"You wouldn't want to be a bra manufacturer," my

mother observed. "There's so much variety in the shapes and sizes of breasts."

My father was trying to set up some deals with an American businessman named Donald Burns, who was staying in Jos for a few months. Donald must have liked kids because he and I spent many hours playing Monopoly. After horseback riding, Monopoly was my favorite thing to do. I loved accumulating property and money, collecting $200 as I passed Go, getting rent money, buying houses and hotels, and bankrupting my opponents. I would laugh, growing richer or poorer, having so much

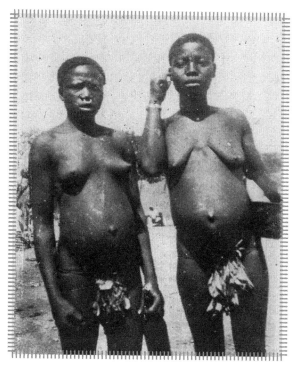

"You wouldn't want to be a bra manufacturer"

fun that I couldn't tear myself away, and the games would last for hours.

Occasionally, my parents and I would drive out to the bush to visit my father's tin mines. On the drive to and from the mines, we played Geography and counted anthills. Once when we stopped to stretch our legs we couldn't get out of the car because we spotted a pack of bush dogs. There were about fifteen of them, tan with black snouts, snarling, scary-looking animals that looked like dogs from hell. Off in the distance we would sometimes see a dog-faced baboon, alone in a field.

In a photograph from one of those trips I'm wearing dungarees and a sleeveless blouse. I'm slender and my dark brown hair is long and wavy under a baseball cap and I'm wearing sunglasses. On this trip I met the emir who owned the mine and gave him some presents my father had brought for his eight-year-old daughter. Despite wearing my baseball cap for protection from the sun, by evening I was nauseous and feverish from sunstroke.

We joined the Plateau Club, which was for whites only. We hung out there on weekends, sitting on a stool at the bar, with me drinking an orange squash and my father smoking an endless succession of non-filtered cigarettes and entertaining me by blowing smoke rings. I took out books from the club library, climbed the large, graceful tree at the front door, and spent afternoons reading Agatha Christie mysteries, watching from above as club members came and went.

Every Sunday we had lunch in the club's tiny restaurant, where they always served a hot Indian curry with at least ten accompaniments. After lunch we played snooker on the oversized six by twelve-foot table, or watched a snooker tournament.

At Christmas the English children flew down to Nigeria from their boarding schools and the club had a costume party for them. Most of the children were dressed up in sweet, cute costumes, but my mother dressed me up as Abe Lincoln. From somewhere she got a mask of Lincoln, not at all sweet or cute, dressed me in dungarees and borrowed a shotgun for me to carry. I know that I scared at least one little girl who was dressed up as Little Bo Peep, because I have a photo of her recoiling in fear from me.

The grownups had their costume parties, too. These events were anticipated for weeks and everyone participated and dressed up as something fanciful. My mother created one costume by sewing hundreds of paillettes on a magenta wool cape she had made. She looked so pretty when they kissed me good-bye and went off to the dance at the club, leaving me alone in the hotel room.

When I awoke later that night in the darkened room, they were still gone. I couldn't get back to sleep and I began to worry that there was a lion under my bed. I had just heard people talking about a leopard attack on some hunters and it scared me because the leopard had torn off one of the men's ears. The woman who was telling the story said, "The poor dear leopard didn't have a chance." I knew there really was no way a lion or leopard could have been in the room; it was upstairs in a hotel that was in town, not out in the bush, but I couldn't banish the thought. I wanted to turn on the light, but I was afraid to step on the floor because the lion under the bed might get me, so I jumped about five feet from my bed to my mother's, reached the light switch, and left it on until they came back.

The next day my mother told me what everyone had worn, like the woman who shocked the other guests by wearing lit candles on her hat to look like a birthday cake. I never told her about my fear that a lion was in the room.

On the weekend we went to the cinema on whites-only night. We saw the coronation of Queen Elizabeth in a weeks-old newsreel, and Tarzan movies we thought were hilarious because they were so different from our reality. No one swung from trees; in Jos there was no jungle and barely any trees at all. On other nights we saw *Frances the Talking Mule*, with Donald O'Connor, a Burl Ives movie, and two pirate movies with Errol Flynn. It seemed like it would be fun and romantic to be kidnapped by him.

One night it rained while we were in the theater and, as we left, we saw that the rain had brought out the "sausage flies"—huge, fat, hideous flying insects that were attracted to the street lamps. Like moths, they flew at the lights and died. They fell to the ground at the foot of the lamp poles and there were mounds of them, some two feet high. The Africans swept them up to take home and cook to eat with their gari, a kind of cereal.

Horseracing and betting were a big part of the socializing in Jos, so many of our weekends were spent at the track. A lot of the mining people owned racehorses and Africans could enter their horses, too. My parents had an ongoing invitation to sit in the owners' stand, where tea and drinks were served. Everyone went, so we would meet a lot of people we knew and have an inexpensive and exciting afternoon. Even kids could place a bet for sixpence.

Since we were the only Americans in Jos who were neither missionaries nor attached to the American embassy, my father felt that we stuck out like sore thumbs, as did our black power-top Buick. As the British tried to make some sense of who my father was and what he was doing in Nigeria, a number of rumors circulated that friends passed on to him. One was that he represented a wealthy American syndicate and was there to buy up everything and squeeze the British out. That was, of course, untrue, but if it had been true, then he was obviously a man to be feared and he was viewed accordingly. Another rumor was that he had a criminal record in New York and that his name was mud with the banks in Lagos and New York.

He had been careful to steer clear of any rows because of the danger that he might be considered a disturbing element and be forced to leave the country. He had too much time and money invested there to run that risk; it would have been foolhardy to jeopardize everything on account of malicious gossip.

Then, at a dance at the club one night, my father had drunk one pink gin too many when he heard the rumor that his family had black blood. "While I don't care one way or the other about the latest rumor, Josie," he said, "the time has come to stop the wagging tongues. I can still flatten most men."

"Lee," my mother cautioned, "just because you boxed at Brown twenty years ago doesn't mean you're still in shape." Nevertheless, over my mother's objections, he handed her his wristwatch and approached the first rumor-monger.

"You have a big mouth and a long tongue," my father said. "I'm sick of all the lies you've been telling about me. You can have it inside the club or outside, your option."

The man had been talking to a group of people, but at this outburst from my father, conversation abruptly halted. As everyone watched aghast, the man turned pale and stammered, "Lee, I assure you I have nothing but the highest regard for your family and America. Actually, I hope we'll be friends. Let me buy you a drink, old chap."

"No thanks," my father replied. "Just watch your mouth," and he marched back to where my mother had been holding her breath as she watched the scene unfold.

He had another drink to bolster his courage. Then, despite my mother's warning him again, "You're not as young as you used to be," he went looking for the next "wicked gossiper." He gave him the same choice: "Inside or outside."

He got the same response from the second man and, returning to his table, he had another drink. By now he was more than angry; he was belligerent. He sought out four more prospects, but found no takers. After that evening, the gossip undoubtedly continued, probably even accelerated, but never reached my father's ears again.

Chapter 22

▼▼ ▼▼ ▼▼ ▼▼ ▼▼

Letter to Hen

July 4, 1952

Dear Hen,

It's July Fourth today, but there are no fire-works going off here. The Brits are still angry with America for the Boston Tea Party and the whole colony thing, but obviously, they wouldn't be cel-ebrating our independence from them anyway. There's a small party at the American Embassy to-night, but very low key. It should be fun, and it's a chance to get dressed up and see people.

Every time we think we see progress with the mines, something catastrophic happens to bring us down to earth and we're back at the beginning again, but deeper in debt. My opinion is that soon-er or later we'll have to close the mines. Maybe that won't be so bad since Lee's not having any more luck at getting the galena and tin than the emir does. We could just buy it from the emir and then Lee wouldn't have to spend so much time in the bush. Of course, I try to keep these thoughts to myself—I don't want to bring him down by being negative. Or is it being realistic?

I guess I'm sounding a little down. I hope I have better news to report in my next letter. I'll write again as soon as I can.

All my love to you, Steve, and the girls,
Josie

Chapter 23

▼▼▼▼▼

The Mines and T. L. Diamond

I'm driving down to our new galena mine next week," my father wrote to Sidney. "I'm taking Animashaun, three stewards, my manager Miles, and the new prospector. If we're lucky we might find silver and maybe even a little gold in the lead. This could be really big!"

My father found out the hard way just how difficult it would be to reach the new site the following week when he and his men drove down as far as the road could take them. They parked the pickup truck on the side of the road and went the rest of the way off-road seven miles over fields and streams on bike and foot. It seemed like a never-ending trek in the heat with no shade and no road, just dry landscape strewn with rocks and brush, every-one shouldering his share of the equipment that would be needed for the next three weeks.

The three stewards carried fifteen whiskey bottles filled with water, a water filter, a canvas bathtub and washstand, several Coleman pressure lamps, kerosene, tins of food including Campbell's soup, Spam, and corned beef hash, clothing, and other personal items. When they arrived at the site of the future mine, the stewards immediately got busy unpacking and setting up the camp. They built a fire to boil water from a nearby stream, and then poured the boiled water into a slow-dripping filter. This process was continued until the traveling water supply was replenished and there was sufficient drinking water for several days. A steward served tea to my father as soon as the water was ready.

As the sun began to set, a steward prepared my father's bath. The "tub" was a folding canvas affair, four feet square and about six inches deep, which rested on the ground. It seemed utterly ridiculous to my father to bathe in the little canvas and frame contraption, yet, as he had occasion to realize many times in the bush, you can get used to anything.

By the time he completed his bath, the steward had laid out "proper" clothing for dinner, including a shirt and tie to replace the bush jacket and shorts my father been wearing during the day. When he had finished dressing, a Scotch and water awaited him.

The local emir had sent over chickens and vegetables and eggs that the stewards cooked over an open fire. Later, when my father would tell this story, and he did many times, he never changed or embellished it. It was the truth and that was enough. You could smell the smoke and the chicken cooking, as he savored the memory of the taste, and the experience of a campfire in the dark African night, far, far away from New York. Nearby, in the blackness outside the camp were naked pagans with bows and arrows, drums throbbing in the distance.

He was beyond the last outpost of civilization, yet here he was, wearing a white shirt and tie, his shoes freshly shined, refreshed from a bath and feeling pretty good after a couple of drinks while looking over week-old airmail

Hausa village chief

editions of the *New York Times* and the *New York Herald Tribune* from Paris, that he had brought with him.

Dinner was completed with a cup of Nescafé to which the steward added a dash of brandy. The proceedings were so ceremonious that it was ten o'clock by the time the meal was over. The evening ended with my father catching up on the news with an overseas broadcast of the BBC on his shortwave radio. He then crawled onto his folding army cot of canvas and wooden legs, and shortly after the steward settled the DDT-sprayed mosquito netting around him, he fell asleep under the stars.

The next morning began at the crack of dawn when the steward brought a tea tray, waking my father by yanking out the tucked-in net, and taking his daytime shoes out to be shined. By the time he was shaved, washed, and dressed, breakfast was ready. The cook had prepared a paw paw melon, fried eggs accompanied by a stewed tomato, toast with marmalade, and a cup of Nescafé.

The emir had said that he could provide all the workers my father would need. On the first day, six laborers were hired to build a one-room mud-walled hut for my father and to begin work on a camp for the mineworkers. None of the workers spoke English, but Animashaun was able to translate my father's orders. By the end of the week there were sixty-five workers and he assigned some of them to build a road and bridges for easier travel between the mine and the main road. The remaining workers opened up a wide pit for the mine and built steps around the sides to prevent landslides.

While the men dug, pagan women, some wearing a

At the mines

sarong, and most wearing only a thong and some leaves, carried the sand and minerals up out of the mine in calabashes on their heads or shoulders. When they reached the top where my father and the manager were waiting, the ore was separated from the soil and rock, leaving an ever-growing pile of small stones. The galena was then stored in a nearby locked shed. It was hard work for fourteen cents a day.

My father was hoping for fifty tons of galena the first month and one hundred tons a month from then on. But most of August, the work at the mine was slowed by an insufficient number of workers and rain filling up the pits. It always rained heavily at least once a day until the end of the rainy season, sometime in October. The men would remove the overburden and expose the lode, and then the rain would come down and the dirt would cover it again. Or they would hit some galena and dig it out, and then it would abruptly end.

"Just a few feet deeper," my father said to himself. "We're only about fifteen feet from the surface." He said this, even though he had previously estimated that the galena was only two to eight feet down.

Building the road and bridges to the mine was going slowly, but my father felt that he couldn't complain too much. After all, he wasn't being charged for the road-building labor since he'd given the emir a ram as a present. However, the district officer, who was a friend of my father's, showed up at the mine and got after the laborers. Three weeks later, when my father was ready to return to Jos, a seven-mile road had been made and nineteen bridges and culverts had been built. It was an extraordinary feat considering the primitive tools they had at their disposal. My father left Animashaun in charge at the mine with the feeling that things were well under control.

Fed up with being constantly underfunded by his partners' lack of action when he needed money to make purchases, my father had written to them, terminating the relationship. That got their attention, and they finally responded, demanding that he call them. This was impossible because there was no phone service from Jos to New York, only from Lagos, which was an eight-hundred-mile plane trip away. The partners claimed that he owed them

Hard work

$25,000, which my father disputed. He said the amount was less than $10,000.

To Sidney he wrote that he knew he still owed him and their mother $2,000, but before he paid them back, he would need another $2,000 to keep himself afloat. He was sure that the first fifty tons from his mine would put him on his feet, and after that he would be able to pay back *all* the money he owed.

In what seemed like a lucky break, a metallurgist named T.L. Diamond, who had heard about my father from my father's other brother Dan, wrote expressing interest in getting in on his mining business. Diamond was planning on flying over from America to discuss it. My father was hopeful that they might be able to form some kind of partnership, but as time went on, and Diamond kept sending cables postponing his date of departure, he began to think that Diamond wasn't too stable and wouldn't be good to do business with.

My father's premonition about T.L. Diamond was confirmed when he finally did show up in Jos. I got my first glimpse of him when we came downstairs to greet him as he was checking in at the Pax Hotel. I thought he looked like a weasel. Instead of holding out his hand to shake, he handed my father a bill for some things he had brought over for my parents. Prior to coming to Nigeria, Diamond had offered to bring anything my parents might need and my father had had various items sent over to Diamond's office, but he had left a lot of things, like medicine for my mother, back in New York.

Diamond spent only one night at the Pax. The next day, saying the hotel was "repulsive," he switched to the Hill Station, taking his ascots, knee socks, and safari jackets with him. On his second evening my parents offered to take him to the movies or the club to watch a big billiard match, but he declined, saying they didn't need to entertain him.

He took my father's check from a New York bank for the items he had brought, three days later he demanded local currency, and when my father offered him local currency, he turned it down saying he didn't want to get stuck with it when he left. In a quandary as to how to satisfy this man, my father said he'd cash local currency for him back into dollars whenever he liked and Diamond answered, "I'll think about it."

"That guy Diamond is a jerk and a swine, if ever I saw one—about the worst I've ever met," my father complained to Sidney. "He thought he could set up a get-rich quick scheme, so he ran all over Jos, meeting with people I've never been able to see, but he didn't get anywhere with them. He thought the miners would sell to him, but he didn't understand that they sell directly to the smelter and didn't need *him* as a middleman. He refused to go to see my mine because he didn't want to travel into the countryside and sleep outside and maybe get a little dirty. And he accused me of not having a real business.

"He arrived August 4th and pulled out August 13th," my father fumed. "Good riddance to him and I hope his plane cracks up!" And thus ended all hope for outside help.

My father said that if he made a pile of money, he might build a house for us or anyone who took his place when we left. He applied to the government for a plot of one and a half acres to build a house with sweeping views of the countryside, across the road from my school. The rent for the land was $22 a year, and the lease could be renewed forever. However, the department in charge of granting permission for the land and house was reluctant to give him a permit because they said they were trying to discourage "ribbon development." They said this, despite the fact that, once outside the township of Jos, the landscape was almost completely devoid of buildings. It was pretty obvious the government was trying to prevent them from leasing the land and building a house.

In a letter to Sidney my father said he was thinking of selling the mines to his own company for about $50,000. He said he would call that his capital investment when he started earning some money. That way the first $50,000 wouldn't be counted as income and he and my mother could draw salaries, and he could pile on travel and all other kinds of business expenses and get semi-free trips to Europe and New York. "In addition, if the company owns the house, we can take depreciation as a tax deduction. What do you think of the idea?" he asked Sidney.

Sidney responded, "Although your progress at the mines appears to be slow, I'm glad that you're making some headway and hope that things will perk up soon. Are you figuring on coming back?" he added. "If so, when?"

With Sidney bearing down on him about coming home and about his profit margins, my father realized that, until he had some actual experience and knew the daily and monthly production, and the cost of production, it was academic to try to figure the profits. But if the potential was considered, then, to my father, who needed to have his fantasies, it conservatively figured to make $100 a ton.

My father's prospector went to see the next area he was staking, where the lode was thought to be quite a bit larger than at the first mine. But when the prospector arrived he was scared off by a wild buffalo and a hyena. Wild buffalo, known as bush cows, are said to be one of the most dangerous animals in the world to hunt, because if you merely wound them, they are known to disappear into the bush and circle around and hunt *you.*

My parents began to talk of going to Europe and New York. Of course, as my father said, it was a dream, until he made "some real money." By October, my father, who must have been getting very homesick, said, "You know, Jo, we should think about trying to get Dan to come here. He's a nice guy and gets along well with everyone." Of course, Dan knew nothing about their plan for him and his young family to relocate to Africa.

"Once this thing is organized and has regular production, Dan will be able to run it and won't make any more mistakes than I do," my father said.

"You know what I'd love to do?" my mother asked. "I'd love to stop off in Europe for a while before heading for New York!"

Yes, I thought. Yes, to Europe and most especially to America! Boy, was I homesick!

My father agreed. "I think the nicest thing to do would be to fly to Europe and then take a boat back to the States. But I guess there's no use making any plans when there's no money to carry them out."

Meanwhile, before the fantasy of Dan coming to run the mines and rescue us from this hellhole could take hold, the lead market took a terrible nosedive.

Chapter 24

More Problems

Despite the new problem of the lead market tanking, my father still felt he could make plenty of money if he operated more efficiently. He hired a new man for less money who he hoped would be a better manager, an African this time, and staked out a tin mine near the lead mine. With tin selling for much higher prices than lead, and what he felt were pretty good tin reserves, he was optimistic that this time he would strike it rich.

"It's a lot of sweat, worry, headache and a little blood," he said to my mother, "but it's definitely worth the candle."

Even though he had told Diamond that he intended to devote himself solely to mining, he began to trade in beeswax and skins. He arranged some purchases with a young Frenchman from the adjoining Cameroons who had come to Jos to trade—that is, if the Frenchman survived the five-day truck trip back to the Cameroons with an appendix that was kicking up.

"From what you say about opening a new mine," Sidney wrote, "it seems to me that you intend to remain in Africa for a long time. Just what are your plans? Are you staying there or returning to this country?"

"Dear Sid," my father answered. "When you have problems or aren't feeling well, unless there's something physically wrong, the solution is easy—just put as much money in the bank as possible. The more you have, the better you'll feel. When I had $40,000 in the bank, my back stopped hurting me, I didn't get any colds, I stopped coughing, nothing irritated me, I slept much better, and felt fine generally. There's nothing like a good bank balance for your nervous system. You remember that I passed out one night in my bedroom in Jackson Heights when I was broke and worried so much about it that I couldn't sleep and got sick over it.

"Re staying in Africa—I think the place to be is where you make your living and you have a few friends. If you have enough money you can be comfortable and happy anywhere. There's no such opportunity for me in New York as I have here to make a lot of money—the real velvet comes when you operate your own mine. The people here spend all they make though they make a lot, but I didn't come here for fun—I want to pile up all the dough I can in a short time. So, in response to your letter, I have no intention of returning except if I go completely broke and can't make money here, or when I make a lot and can take a trip home."

My father also began asking friends and relatives in the States to do transactions for him behind his partners' back, and he started a trading company that he named Sevenoaks, after the town where I had gone to school in England. He justified this secret company by saying that his partners had let him down, that he had been *forced* to proceed secretly because his partners had been so unreliable about keeping him in funds to make purchases and he wasn't making enough money to live on.

"You know, Josie," he told my mother, "business is a little different from the practice of law. If a businessman starts splitting hairs, he'll never accomplish anything. I think there's a bit of the desperado in most successful business men."

Sidney wrote, "If you terminate your dealings with your partners now, where will you get the capital to continue operating? If your partners won't provide you with money, and you don't have your own, the only solution is for you to return home."

"Dear Sid," my father replied in yet another letter full of details used to bolster his optimism. "Here's my picture: I have $4700 in cash of which $2300 is my partners', leaving a balance of $2400. Of this, I owe you and Mom $2000, so I have $400 of my own. But I also have nineteen tons of galena purchased with my own money. It cost me $2200 and has a value in New York of $5700, so you can see that I am just on the point of being able to swing it without my partners—particularly as I intend to ship twenty of their tons which I have here to England; thus I will have the proceeds of that batch for operations, so that I am free of my partners. Those twenty tons will bring me $6000 and set me up with my own nineteen.

"Of course, I'll have to sweat a little until I get paid for the stuff I have," he continued, "but it's worth it, because then I'll be independent."

Sidney responded in his usual tone, trying to bring my father back down to earth and see things for what they really were.

"Dear Lee," he wrote. "I have your letter and am glad that you appear to be progressing. But don't forget that since your partners paid for the twenty tons, some of the $6000 is theirs and is owed to them."

Bewildered by my father's lack of mining success, my parents discussed how the other small private tin mine operators made a living; some of them only mined two tons a month, and still managed to "live like kings" with a couple of cars, horses and servants.

My father told my mother that mining was easy. For tin it was essential to have a three-quarter-ton truck to transport a few men and equipment, and for galena you needed to have one or more five-ton trucks. He had already purchased picks, shovels, survey instruments, head pans, buckets, and ropes. Unfortunately, he didn't have money to buy trucks or any of the heavy-duty equipment that the large mining companies used.

"I'm not going to settle down in this damn place," my father wrote to Sidney. "I just want to get an organization rolling, then maybe someone else can take over and we can go back to civilization for a while."

Then he asked for another $2000. "It's a small amount but makes a heck of a big difference," he wrote, "and I don't expect I'll need it again." More than a year and a half after my parents had arrived in Africa, my father was still short on working capital, and was once again down to his last $400.

Chapter 25

▽▽▽ ▽▽▽ ▽▽▽ ▽▽▽ ▽▽▽

Letter to Hen

Aug. 15, 1952
Dear Hen,

I'm enclosing a great photo of Alida and me. This is what it's really like—the pagan women really are walking around naked—but I just love the picture with Alida and me juxtaposed next to them. Alida's been drawing pictures of naked women. I hope it doesn't affect her psyche.

I've gotten friendly with a freelance government photographer, who's Hungarian. He's handsome and fun to spend time with and it gives me something interesting to do. Several weeks ago Alida and I accompanied him on a day trip in the bush. He's been hired by the government to take pictures of the natives and the countryside. It was very hot that day and that's why Alida looks so wilted. Also, there is a picture of us with a twelve-

Jo and Alida

year-old boy in front of a huge rock that looks like
it could just go rolling down the hill at any moment.
And the scary one of us on the "swinging bridge."
It really did swing and sway as we crossed over
it and when we looked down, the gorge was way,
way below us.

    Hans, the photographer, does something that
I don't quite approve of, and that is letting Alida
steer the car from the middle seat next to him,
while he controls the speed. I allow it because she

gets so much pleasure and excitement from it, and because the road is empty of traffic most of the time. She has the unfortunate habit of letting go of the wheel suddenly if she sees another car coming toward us, but he told her not to do that and she has

Jo and Alida on the swinging bridge

pretty much stopped. I think that at the age of nine a lifelong love of driving has been born in her.

I'm sorry I didn't write sooner, but I was very sick for about a week and so was Alida. Lee was away at the mine for about three weeks, and we were all alone in the hotel in Jos. We were so sick, with all the symptoms of malaria, that eventually I had to ask the owner of the hotel to drive us to the hospital. They took multiple x-rays of my stomach but couldn't decide what I had, and they couldn't figure out what was wrong with Alida, who was also sick with fever and pains so severe they thought she might have rheumatism. Finally they just called it "Jos Tummy" for both of us. I guess that's what they call any problems they can't diagnose.

We were in the hospital for about a week. It was so awful with Lee away, to be sick and completely on our own, and no way of contacting him. We're fine now, but it makes me wish more than ever that we were back in the States. At least, if the mining were going well, it might possibly be worth the pain and travail, but it's not working out so far.

Alida seems happy in school, and she's training for a couple of events in the gymkhana (a horse show). Every day, weather permitting, we drive her over to the polo field, and she practices for the events in which she'll be riding. I have my heart in my mouth because the little pony bucks now and then for no apparent reason, but so far, she's managed to hang on. She's a good rider and riding is her greatest joy.

Well, dear, that's all for now. Hope you are all well.

Love,
Josie

Chapter 26

The End is Near

Desperate for my father to return to America, Sidney wrote that he had found a business on Long Island for my father to take over. He said that a client named Raymond had an electrical contracting business on Long Island that he just couldn't handle any more. The business netted about $50,000 a year, but Raymond was sick and tired of it. He wanted to devote himself to building houses in Connecticut and would be willing to sell it for $50,000.

"It would merely require common sense and hard work," Sidney wrote. "If you're interested in it, let me know how much money you could put up and if you could raise any money from your in-laws."

The notion of raising money from my father's in-laws was ridiculous, considering that Sidney knew he was the person who had been keeping my father afloat for the past year and a half. He knew better than anyone that we were broke, and also that my mother's father, who had made and lost several fortunes, had died while we were in Africa, so *he* wasn't going to invest.

In July of 1952 I entered fifth grade at Hillcrest, still in the same classroom, just over one row. In November we went to a party at the home of missionaries who had just come back from leave in America. It was the night of the Eisenhower–Stevenson election, and as we waited to hear the returns over a shortwave radio, our hosts amazed us with the lightweight aluminum lounge chairs they had brought back from America. Aluminum, a portent of things to come—aluminum, a competitor of tin, although we didn't know it then.

In December at the Christmas party, the Plateau Club played a record of Bing Crosby singing "White Christmas" and our longing for America became almost unbearable. I missed my cousins and friends terribly and couldn't wait to get back to the States. We all had to fight back tears.

A few weeks after Sidney's suggestion that my father become an electrical contractor, Sidney brought up the subject of Raymond Electric again. My father replied that he was interested, "in principle, but I'm inclined to be skeptical over the reasons the guy gives for wanting to sell." And, in one of his rare lucid business assessments, he added, "No one gets disgusted with a business that nets $50,000 a year. There must be more to it than that."

The mining business had deteriorated to the point that he closed up his lead mine just before Christmas, since it had drained all the profit he was making on the lead he was buying from the African chief.

Undaunted by his failures, and increasingly desperate

to make money and stay afloat, my father now staked out claims for five tin mines and was waiting for leases to be granted by the government so he could begin mining them. He said to my mother that tin was quite different to mine than lead because the reserves could be accurately estimated and the laborers were paid piecework for the number of pounds they turned in, "so you only pay for what you get."

We were sitting in the lounge upstairs at the Pax, a few doors away from our bedrooms, and my mother was teaching me some new embroidery stitches for a tablecloth I was working on.

"Frankly," he said to my mother, "I'm pessimistic that they'll approve my applications. The British are such bastards! They're afraid and jealous of Americans and they do everything they can to obstruct me." In my father's vacillation between euphoria and despondency, he failed to recognize that he had been spectacularly unsuccessful thus far, causing my mother to wonder what he thought the British were jealous of.

"Meanwhile," he continued, "I'm winding up all prospecting and I'm not going to do anything further until I hear from the government regarding the leases. If they grant them, I'll begin mining tin. Once I get it organized, we can leave this place. I thought I could make a quick pile and return to New York, but now I see it can't be done fast."

"It might take months to get the leases, and why would you start mining tin if we're going to leave?" my mother asked.

He ignored her comment and said, "While I'm waiting to hear from the government, I'll continue buying lead ore from the chief, and after a few months we'll return to New York. The thing is, if we leave here right now, I'll lose everything I've put into the mines because they'll be impossible to sell. If people know you're leaving, why should they buy them? They can just wait for you to go.

"The best I can hope for is to make a deal with someone else here to run them for a cut of the profits. And then expect to get gypped unmercifully. But," he added hopefully, "I might get *some* income out of it."

There was a long pause while they considered the implications of going home broke and getting into a business my father knew nothing about. After a while, my father wondered aloud, "Is electrical contracting a dying field, or are there as many jobs available as when Raymond started the business?"

He wrote Sidney that he would cast the die about coming home in a few weeks. "I want to keep trading for a few months, then leave this place with around $15,000 of my own and have Animashaun carry on here, as he can do it without me. Right now I feel very optimistic about making money for the next few months with the chief's ore. That's what's kept us going the last few months."

However, following the closing of my father's mine, he was experiencing difficulty getting the galena from the chief's mine, too, and by the end of February, even those deliveries ended. He had gotten permission to operate the tin mines he had staked out, but they weren't doing much better, with the tin coming out in a trickle.

He asked Sidney to get him a complete description of Raymond's electrical business and all the figures. Meanwhile, he proceeded with tin mining as if the conversation about ending it had never occurred. He built a mining camp and housing for the laborers at the mine, and recruited a batch of men, hoping to get a ton of tin a month. He was sure that production would increase as he got more leases.

"Sometimes I'm way down in the dumps and sometimes I'm very hopeful," he wrote to Sidney. "Life here is alternately dreary and very interesting. We would consider it first-class if we only had a house to live in and it seems the only way we can get one is to build it. I think I can put up something for not much more than $2,000. But I'm not going to spend a cent until I'm way ahead of the game—though it would save me a lot of money versus what we pay for the hotel, with three of us in two rooms and all meals. Actually, it's not too bad, except that the hotel itself, located right at the edge of the native part of town, isn't so hot."

In his next letter, Sidney wrote that, contrary to what he originally had thought, the electrical contracting business was in a very bad state and he was trying to work out a deal with Raymond's creditors. "Sidney told Raymond," my father reported to my mother, "that if he closed the company down in its present situation, bankruptcy would follow and the stigma would be attached to him, so they're trying to get the creditors to hold off until they find someone else to take over the business."

It was a Saturday afternoon, and the three of us were playing snooker at the club. My mother was about to take her shot, but this remark from my father brought her up short. "Lee," my mother said, "if the debts are merely postponed, doesn't that mean that the next owner inherits them? Why is that a good deal for *you*?" She lined up a red ball and dropped it in the corner pocket. She missed her next shot and my father chalked up his cue.

"Sidney says that the business went to hell because Raymond began to devote more time to the housing project and ignored the electrical business," he replied. "When he couldn't meet his obligations, he handed out a number of phony financial statements and generally loused himself up in the trade. He thinks this is a great opportunity for me because he knows that I'm a hard worker and would really devote myself to turning the company around. They're going to try to get the larger creditors to hold off. Raymond would work with me in the business for one or two months and then turn it over."

"So, now that he acknowledges he's in big trouble, he comes to Sidney, hat in hand," my mother said, "and he wants to give the business away, so *his* bankruptcy stigma becomes *yours*! All Raymond wants is to get way from it and be sure that it won't fold until after he leaves. He doesn't care what happens to *you*," my mother said in an exasperated tone. "And one or two months is barely any time at all to learn a whole new business!"

"Sidney said that Raymond finally got an accountant in last weekend who came up with some tentative figures that show Raymond owes over $200,000 to his trade creditors. But he says I shouldn't look a gift horse in the mouth."

"Lee," my mother said, "what kind of gift is this? How are you going to pay off $200,000 in one year? Plus pay your salary, the rent for the business, the employees, and purchase new inventory?" She had managed to keep her mouth shut about all my father's financial misadventures, but now she was worried.

My father replied, "Sidney thinks Raymond will be able to collect enough from his accounts to take care of the smaller creditors and keep the business going. And he also thinks there'll be plenty of people who would be interested in taking over the company if I don't want it. Raymond's anxious to get away because this is the building season and Sidney says if I continue to stall I can forget about the whole thing. He says Raymond can't suit my convenience."

He added, almost dreamily, "I don't think there's any mystery about running the business. I think if Sidney can get it for me, I ought to take it. Sidney said that if we work the deal out, it's possible Raymond would suddenly decide he wants some payment, but he feels that's just a detail."

"Sidney!" my mother exploded. "I don't think he's looking after you. What's so great about a bankrupt business and a mountain of debt? I want to go home more than anything, but I don't think this is a good way to do it. And," she added, "what's that supposed to mean—Raymond might suddenly decide he wants payment—what kind of a *detail* is that?"

To Hen she wrote, "Both Lee and Sidney are Phi Beta Kappa from Brown, and Yale Law School graduates. Two smart men, so why would they think this is a good idea? Who is Sidney representing—Lee or Raymond? How will Lee handle $200,000 in debt? And how will Lee, the lawyer, suddenly become an electrical contractor?

"Our social life is almost non-existent, I miss you and the girls. I miss Saks and Lord & Taylor. Sarah wrote that she looks across the garden for our cats on the windowsill and misses me. And I miss America. But if Lee takes on this bankrupt company, how will we survive?"

My father wrote Sidney with a list of questions about Raymond Electric. Sidney wrote back that he understood my father having so many questions but that he couldn't answer them. According to Raymond, the business could be rebuilt and my father should be able to make $20,000 a year, plus a car, *once it got on an even keel*. But Sidney also said that, while Raymond believes he is telling the truth, he couldn't if he tried.

In a masterpiece of understatement Sidney wrote, "If you want this business, you take it entirely at your own risk. There will be a lot of headaches, heartaches, and hard work, not only because the business is tough, but because you'll be taking over a particularly difficult situation with all kinds of unknown liabilities." Did this signal a challenge to my father that he couldn't resist?

"If you want to do a deal you'll have to do it quickly,"

Sidney continued, "because Raymond is anxious to get away. Maybe you should come here alone to look things over. Then if it looks OK, you can bring your family and give up your mines. Or you can go back; your only loss in that case will be your fare, plus some time off from the mines. Let me know right away."

Chapter 27

Letter to Hen

Feb. 1953

Dear Hen,

Guess what! We might be coming home soon! From a selfish standpoint, I've about had it here. Three bouts with malaria, living in this hole, bathroom down the hall and sharing a small room with Alida. Also, things at the mines are worse.

A bankrupt electrical supply and contracting business for free gives me pause, but Lee seems to feel like he might be able to make it work. Sidney's been trying to get more information from the owner of the business, and pending that, I think we'll be coming back.

Your sister has become a pretty good snooker player. We learned to play on a huge six by twelve-foot table, and if you can play on that, you can play on anything. Though I'll miss snooker match-

es and the adventure of living in Africa (it certain-ly has been a novel two years), America is where my heart is.

I hope that Eisenhower will be a good presi-dent. I would have voted for Stevenson if we had been home—I think he's much smarter than "Ike."

I can't wait to see you and the girls! I'm still sad that I couldn't go to Father's funeral and that I wasn't there when he died. I'll let you know more when I know more, but keep your fingers crossed.

Love,

Josie

Chapter 28

▼▼▼▼▼

Getting Out

Sidney, I'm in a financial hole due to poor deliveries of galena from the emir in January, February, and March," my father wrote, sounding a familiar theme.

He reported that the six and a half tons he had finally been able to get (when he had been hoping for 100 tons) were finally on their way from the mine, but would probably miss the ship on which they were booked.

"So I'm short of cash. If you can accommodate me with a loan, Sid, when I get paid for some of the stuff already shipped, I'll pay you back right away, and also something for the past loan, so that your advance will be outstanding for a very short time.

"I'm trying to wrap things up here," he continued, "but we're finding out that, even as a gift, it's not so easy to get rid of Alida's pony." I was sad about giving up Pixie, but my excitement for returning to America helped to mitigate the loss. I liked him but I had never loved him the way I loved Beauty in that forever kind of way.

Even though we were coming home, we were getting our teeth fixed up by "a very good English dentist," my father wrote. "We're in excellent shape, luckily, but beginning to pine for New York."

A few days later the three of us were sitting upstairs in the lounge at the Pax, my mother petting Ginger's fluffy orange fur as he curled in her lap purring. I was working on embroidering a pink tablecloth with red and white stars and suns, and my parents were discussing our return to America.

Taking a puff on his cigarette my father said, "It takes a little time for an idea to sink in and to make a decision. I guess I'm psychologically ready to return to New York and take up the electrical business. I just need to get some kind of picture of what I'm getting into. Once the decision is made, we can leave the beginning of May, stop off in Europe for a couple of weeks and then take a boat to America."

He said he had been hesitant about going into the electrical business, but now he was interested because it seemed to offer a chance for hard work and some reward. "And I'm tired of this place with a lot of lousy limeys and a lousy hotel," he concluded.

Sidney asked my father to call him to discuss the deal, but my father told him that the nearest international telephone was 800 miles away, in Lagos. Sidney kept pressing him to come home for a look at Raymond Electric before making a final decision, but my father told him that it wasn't practical to leave my mother and me alone in Africa. He didn't have the money to go back and forth, he said, and besides, Africa was a dangerous place. "If I leave, we all leave."

"If I come back to New York," he wrote, "it'll have to be win or lose. Try to impress on Raymond that he should be frank, honest, and square with us in view of what we have to go through to pull him out of his hole."

He ignored my mother's warning that he would be

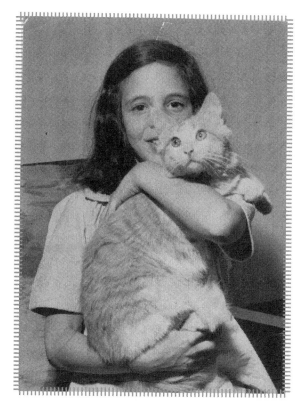

Ginger and Alida in the lounge at the Pax

jumping *into* Raymond's hole. "We can't be there before a few more weeks, so tell Raymond to hang on and not get panicky or crack up." He added, "We're all fine and excited about going back to New York."

"Sidney made an oral deal with Raymond," my father reported to my mother. "He said he couldn't insist on a written contract because Raymond is acting as a friend. Raymond said he would turn the whole business over to me lock, stock, and barrel and do whatever he can to help me."

A few days later Sidney responded to my father's itinerary. "Your reference to leaving in May to go floating around Europe and then taking a boat home shows a complete lack of understanding of the situation. If you want it, take a plane immediately and come over by yourself. Leave your family there until you know it's a go. They can come *after* you. If you can't fly here directly upon receipt of this letter, which would probably get you back here within the next ten days, cable me that you don't want to come at all, so I can advise Raymond. Quit asking for agreements, audits and reports—just come back and take it for what it is.

"Of course, if you were *buying* the business, there would be a real need for checking into Dun and Bradstreet reports, but you aren't buying it, you're getting it as a *gift*. It's a whole lot more than you seem to have now, so I don't see that you have anything to lose."

"Some gift!" my mother interrupted when my father read Sidney's letter to her. "Huge debt—that's why he's 'giving' it away! You *do* have something to lose—your shirt!"

My father cabled Sidney:

IMPRACTICAL TO COME FOR MONTH WITH-
OUT FAMILY

SHOULD HAVE FIRM DEAL BEFORE LEAVING
AS INTEND TO REMAIN UNITED STATES IF WE
RETURN

DEPARTURE SUBJECT CONSUMMATION
AGREEMENT WITH RAYMOND

RENEWING PASSPORTS GETTING INOCULA-
TIONS

EXPECT CLOSE DEAL ON MY MINES SOON

DOING BEST TO EXPEDITE BUT PREMATURE
DEPARTURE DISASTROUS

To my mother he said, "If I go on a test basis, I can't wind up here and meanwhile, everything goes to hell in my absence. Then, if I decide to stay on, everything here is left up in the air. And fare back and forth just to take a look is much too heavy for me right now."

"Why should you go all the way to America just to find out what Sidney could learn in a couple of hours!" she asked him.

Meanwhile, for some reason we were starting to get inoculations, even though we were *leaving* Africa, not *arriving*. Our passports had expired, and my father wired the American consulate in Lagos, asking that new passports be rushed to him. He made arrangements to ship our personal items and the car.

He was still trying to hold Sidney off, writing, "I don't dare leave until my galena is loaded on board a ship. The stuff is worth $4,000 and I'll get sick if it isn't loaded before we leave here. I'm trying to book seats on the plane to Paris. From there, we can go to Copenhagen, then to Helsingborg, Sweden. I'm hopeful I can stir up my old oil burner business, since that's where my best ex-customer is. Then by boat to New York, a five or six day trip.

"We're all excited about coming home," he continued, "and moving as fast as we can at this end. We'll pack our bags the day we get the agreement and know what we're coming back to. I'm trying to wind up as quickly as possible."

My mother read his letter. "Good," she said. "Don't let Sidney stampede you."

We got all our (unnecessary) shots at the hospital, and I was sick in bed with fever from the final one. The ore was being railed down to the port, and we were inching closer to leaving, but Sidney still hadn't sent the requested letter of agreement from Raymond.

In his next letter to Sidney my father wrote, "Subject to getting plane space and our passports back, there is a possibility we can leave Tue. April 21st and be back in New York before the end of the month, provided we get something a little more definite about the deal. Meanwhile, we're continuing our preparations to leave. We're going to have a bad letdown if we don't go because we're figuring on it and talk and think of nothing else. I hope, therefore, that something is in the mail about the stand-by, the credit, and Raymond's letter-agreement."

I was beyond myself with excitement, looking forward to seeing my cousins and returning, finally, to America.

Then two days later, still with no letter of agreement, in a complete turnaround, my father cabled Sidney:

I ACCEPT DEAL YOU MADE WITH RAYMOND TO TAKE BUSINESS LOCK STOCK BARREL

LETTER OF AGREEMENT HIGHLY DESIRABLE

PREPARING TO LEAVE WITH FAMILY AS SOON AS RENEWED PASSPORTS ARRIVE

Epilogue

April 1953

When we arrived in London, my father stopped payment on the check that he had written to Barclays in order to win his release from the police in Kano, and my mother picked up her leopard coat that she had left in storage. Two days later we flew over the English Channel to Paris on one of the most violent and nauseating flights that ever made it without crashing. I wasn't scared, just sick.

After a couple of days sightseeing in Paris with a visit to the Eiffel Tower, and seeing *Bwana Devil*, the hot new 3-D movie about Africa, my father flew to the United States to take over the mess that was Raymond Electric.

My mother and I lingered in Paris at a hotel near the Louvre for two more weeks to give my father time to find a place for us to live. All I wanted to do was get back to America and my cousins, and I was upset that I couldn't leave with my father. I was so disappointed about our extended stay in Paris that even though my mother tried to bribe me with a picture book on cats, and even knowing I was being a brat, I refused to walk across the street and visit the Louvre, which she particularly wanted to do. But finally, the day came that we took the boat train down to Le Havre, where we boarded the SS United States for a stormy five-day trip home.

The morning we arrived in New York I was up and dressed by six. It was dark and foggy, and there were just a few other people on the deck with me. As we floated slowly toward the pier, the Statue of Liberty appeared out of the mist, the most majestic, beautiful sight I've ever seen.

America at last, America of my dreams. I never stopped missing you.

We moved into a garden apartment in Roslyn Heights, Long Island, and in May I entered what was left of fifth grade—about six weeks. The pattern of coming in new and at the wrong time was continuing. I had left Jackson Heights and was returning to Roslyn, and it was hard to walk in to my fourth school in two years. The teacher asked me to speak to a roomful of strangers, my fellow fifth graders, about life in Africa. I did my best and that's how I came to be called "Jungle Baby" by my classmates. I was never quite sure, but I suspected my new nickname wasn't entirely friendly.

We remained in Roslyn until the end of seventh grade, and that's about how long Raymond Electric lasted. My mother never forgave Sidney for getting my father involved with a bankrupt company. After the demise of Raymond Electric, my father went back to doing what he did well and became an outside lawyer for Sidney's bank.

My mother worked with him as his head secretary and office manager when my father opened up his own law office on Long Island, down the street from Saks Fifth Avenue and Lord & Taylor, the stores my mother had written to Hen that she missed. Now Lee Franklin had an office on Franklin Avenue, and a secretary named Alice Franklin. As his practice grew and prospered he hired several young lawyers and we moved to a nice house in the third town in five years.

I was married and pregnant with my second daughter when my mother was diagnosed with pancreatic cancer. While I had been making a baby she had been making a tumor. She died in 1977 after twenty months of suffering, at the age of sixty-nine. My father soldiered on, trying to pursue his law business and some importing and exporting, but he missed my mother terribly. He said he would reach out to touch her in bed but she wasn't there.

We closed up his office and moved it to his house, along with his loyal secretary, Edith, and I arranged for a wonderful young woman to be his housekeeper–caretaker. Much to my shock and anguish, he died one night in his sleep of congestive heart failure, fifteen months after my mother. He was sixty-eight.

My father never lost his passion for foreign trade. At the time of his death he had a shipment of turmeric afloat from a supplier in Haiti. I received word from the Port of New York that the turmeric had arrived, and in the midst of my overwhelming grief, I spent days looking through his files, and made multiple phone calls to locate the buyer and notify him. I got paid the $20,000 that was owed my father, who would have relished both the money and my accomplishment in completing his final business transaction.

Having my own children made me committed to being the best mother I could possibly be. My parents' actions seem even more unjustifiable as time goes on and I view my two daughters and now my four grandchildren through that hurtful lens—they are so small and vulnerable it would be impossible to violate their trusting hearts.

It wasn't until my parents died that the questions I had never asked began to torment me. To this day I don't know what to say about my father. He was a lawyer by profession and a romantic adventurer at heart, but time would prove he was not a realist. For a man struggling to come to terms with an older brother who had gone to the same undergraduate and graduate schools and become very successful, while my father had not, reality was something he preferred to ignore. I know that he was desperate to make a good living and support his family. He saw Africa as his opportunity and was able to justify his actions to Sidney and himself by making up the story that what he did with me was all right because I was happy. He ignored the larger truth that he had twice abandoned his eight-year-old daughter around the world for close to a year.

My mother should have known better. She was extremely critical of my Uncle Steve for placing his daughters in an orphanage at the ages of two and four when their mother, Hen, got throat cancer. They were there for a year or more so that he could continue to work and look after his wife. And my mother had suffered terribly when she was sent to live with her grandmother when *her* own mother was sick.

However, my mother had already learned from experience that my father might abandon her as well, and she feared that more than anything. I guess in the long term she made the right decision for her because there was no way she could have supported the two of us if they had divorced, and that threat seemed to always hover over the marriage.

I know that my parents loved me and each other, and I loved them, but I'm haunted by my not asking them how they could have betrayed and abandoned their only child. They weren't alcoholics or physically or mentally ill, nor was it a wartime situation. This is what I want to say to my mother:

How could you sacrifice your little girl? Why didn't you stand up for me? Why didn't you protect me? You gave me life, loved me, cared for me when I was sick, worried about me, went to my school plays, bought me dolls and made their clothes, framed my pictures, sewed my clothes, decorated my room, taught me how to embroider, play gin rummy, and read. You let me sleep with you when I was scared or worried, and you also knew the pain of abandonment. I needed you, both of you—my parents.

I'm okay now. But I can still cry.

Thanks to friends and editors and people in my writing groups who read my book before it was fit to be read. Never did I hear anything but encouragement.

Alida Albert is a professional interior designer,
a painter, a writer, and an amateur landscape
designer. She lives with her husband in Connecticut,
and her two daughters live in nearby towns with
their families.

Made in the USA
Lexington, KY
29 October 2014